Burt Lancaster

BURT LANCASTER

Robert Windeler

St. Martin's Press
New York

B
L

Library of Congress Cataloging in Publication Data

Windeler, Robert.
  Burt Lancaster.

  1. Lancaster, Burt, 1913-   2. Moving-picture
actors and actresses—United States—Biography.   I. Title.
PN2287.L246W5   1984   791.43′028′0924   [B]   83-27252
ISBN 0-312-10869-9

First Published in Great Britain in 1984 by W. H. Allen & Co. Ltd.

First U.S. Edition

10 9 8 7 6 5 4 3 2 1

37364

For Diane,
Who also remembers when
the Atlantic Ocean was really something

Burt Lancaster

Introduction

IN 1983, THE year he turned seventy, had quadruple bypass coronary surgery, appeared in the movies *Local Hero* and *The Osterman Weekend*, and the re-release of *The Leopard*, Burt Lancaster also paused long enough to pay lavish tribute to his oldest and best friend in the movie business. Although he boasted that he had only been to about three cocktail parties in his thirty-seven years in Hollywood, not only did Lancaster appear at this one for Kirk Douglas, he greeted the guest of honour with a full kiss on the lips. As honorary chairman of the dinner later that evening, at which Douglas received the Albert Einstein Award from Israel's Institute of Technology (Technion), Burt said of his friend Kirk: 'I've worked with him many times over the span of years, and I think I know him pretty well. Let me start by telling you something about him – to begin with, he is the most difficult and exasperating man that I know, except for myself. He fights with his wife, he fights with his children, he fights with the maid, he fights with the cook. God knows, he has fought with me.'

The audience, which included contemporaries like Gregory Peck, Ernest Borgnine and Robert Mitchum, laughed knowingly at this description of the second most impossible male movie star in Hollywood, as the self-admitted most impossible went on to detail the facts of Douglas's life and to announce that both he and his friend were 'very available to make pictures'. When Lancaster was done, Douglas responded, 'I'm glad that years ago I did not desert Burt Lancaster – stood by him in spite of a hacking cough, fought it out with him at the OK Corral. As I listened to my life story, I thought what a wonderful movie it would make – and there is only one person to play it: Burt Lancaster.'

It could happen. Although the two men don't look alike (Kirk has the dimple, Burt the teeth), Lancaster, in his seventy-one films since 1946, has played an astonishing variety of characters, taking a particular delight in casting himself against type. 'I've always tried to vary my roles,' he said, 'it was the only way I could learn my trade without getting labelled.' Thus he has been both weak and heroic, romantic and deadbeat, con-man and courtier, the killer and even the killed. For most of our lifetimes, and over half of his, he has been the quintessential – if independent – movie star. He has sometimes flopped, but never failed to be interesting, or been out of demand or fashion. His leading ladies have ranged from Ava Gardner, Barbara Stanwyck and Katharine Hepburn, to Claudia Cardinale and Susan Sarandon, and even in clearly supporting roles (taken against conventional Hollywood wisdom) opposite Oscar winners Shirley Booth and

Anna Magnani in *Come Back, Little Sheba*, and *The Rose Tattoo*, Lancaster has been memorable.

Possessing an enormous ego, but almost no vanity, he has always felt that 'the play's the thing'. Besides his own Oscar for *Elmer Gantry* in 1960, no fewer than nine other actors (Shirley Booth, Frank Sinatra, Donna Reed, Anna Magnani, David Niven, Wendy Hiller, Shirley Jones, Maximilian Schell and Helen Hayes) have won Academy Awards acting opposite Lancaster, and twelve more have been nominated for Oscars in Burt's pictures (from Barbara Stanwyck to Susan Sarandon).

A very wealthy man, as much by virtue of his efforts as the first serious actor-producer in the 1950s as from his acting, Lancaster did Bernardo Bertolucci's *1900* for nothing, just because the project appealed to him. Another of his directors, Luchino Visconti (*The Leopard*) said of Burt that he was 'very complex – at times autocratic, rude, strong – at times romantic, good, understanding, sometimes even stupid and, above all, mysterious'. Screenwriter Clifford Odets (*Sweet Smell of Success*) said it was 'difficult to think of Lancaster as just one man'.

'I have always been secretive', Lancaster said in explanation, 'I've never been easy with strangers. So it is hard to know what the public has a right to read about me, and what they haven't. I've never really had a consistent image, so I've had no happy fiction to project.'

Yet he kidded his inconsistent image ('I guess I'm the guy who always went to bed with the girl – even if it was after the movie had finished'), and was very analytical about himself, and Douglas, Mitchum, Peck, Borgnine and the other members of the Hollywood Class of 1946: 'What made us different?' he asked. 'We came along in that post-war transition period. Before

[3]

that, if you weren't a character actor like Spencer Tracy, you were a pretty boy leading man such as Robert Taylor or a Gable personality actor. Now you have the Hoffmans, Pacinos, De Niros, great actors all of them, but these days people seem to want to identify with the actors and the role they play. (We would never have been allowed to play that bloated fighter like De Niro did in *Raging Bull*). The audience doesn't look up to them. There's no fantasy, and too little romance.'

For *Birdman of Alcatraz*, Lancaster shaved his head and aged almost forty years, and he never hesitated to submerge himself in an unpleasant or unattractive character. 'I came in at a time when boudoirs and drawing rooms were going out of fashion,' he noted. 'I was part of the new kind of furniture – tougher, less polished, grainier. I think I realised that at the time, but I have always known that I couldn't settle for the expected. I have always wanted to reach out and I always will. That's why I'm considered an uncomfortable bastard to be with. As a hero, the public always wanted me to get the girl; that's what heroes were for then in Hollywood. But I was never very happy being romantic, Valentino-style, so I used to cut down on the clinches and let them imagine I was making it after the final credits. Maybe they could identify with me more on the way home than when the movie was rolling. I think I may have a respectful following, but not an affectionate one.'

There were only a 'handful' of films that 'I liked myself in, and may be remembered for', he said: *From Here to Eternity, Sweet Smell of Success, Elmer Gantry, The Leopard, Atlantic City*. But the international movie-going audience has discovered Lancaster's unique versatility – almost in retrospect – since the 1981 release of the last film. But at least for the last two decades, perhaps

[4]

less consciously for his whole thirty-seven-year movie career, Lancaster had been alternating one serious work with something to say, and one potboiler, to keep his or his company's cash flowing.

His restlessness and resilience were hard, but honestly, come by, as a slum kid from New York's East Harlem who started show business as a Depression-era circus acrobat for three dollars a week in second-hand tights. While he retained his tenement diction, Lancaster also became the cultured art collector and opera buff who lived part time in Rome. The cranky loner was also the dedicated family man. The circus tumbler and frustrated singer became a million-dollar movie star.

At age three-score-and-ten, even the heart patient was back on the track only a fortnight after his bypass operation, jogging to get his early morning juices flowing ('some men use masturbation', he cracked). There was no talk of retirement or even slowing down, only of the future: 'Everything gets harder as you get older,' he admitted. 'It's a problem that we all have to face, in movies, in the theatre, in life. Getting older means a diminishing of curiosity. As long as you are curious, you defeat age. You have to keep looking for new ideas and concepts, because as you get older you ossify somewhat. You have to watch that. You can't throw out everything that went before, of course, but you still have to keep the door open for something new.'

CHAPTER ONE

East Harlem

W HAT IS NOW East Harlem's 'El Barrio' was a lower middle-class neighbourhood of mixed ethnic origins when Burton Stephen Lancaster was born there on 2 November, 1913, in his family's railroad flat. It was a raw Sunday morning, with the wind whipping across the unaccustomedly quiet New York streets from the west, chasing dry autumn leaves along the gutters of East 106th Street. Outside Number 209 East 106th, a small group had gathered expectantly, as they might have in a maternity hospital waiting-room. The men wore black suits because it was Sunday.

James H. Lancaster, by contrast, was in shirt sleeves when he stepped out onto the stoop of his three-storey tenement building to announce what the assembled neighbours and friends had been waiting to hear. 'It's here,' he said, 'and it's a boy. We're calling him Burton Stephen.' 'That's a pretty important-sounding name,' said one bystander, noting that the new baby's older brothers were James and William, and his older sister was Jane. (There was to be a younger sister, Florence, but she died in her second year, leaving Burton to be raised as the baby of the Lancaster family.)

The crowd gathered to await his birth included Italians, Jews and blacks. There were even some East Indians of the Buddhist faith in the neighbourhood. 'We all mixed,' Burt recalled. 'We were flaxen-haired kids, my two brothers, my sister and me, and I guess we really stood out in that community. I was from an Irish-English background, but the Italians used to call me 'Dutch' because they seemed to think we were German. Typically Italian.'

James Lancaster, Snr worked as a postal clerk at the Madison Square Post Office, working up to a top salary of forty-eight dollars weekly as a supervisor, but he claimed to have traced his ancestry back to Britain's royal House of Lancaster. His wife, of Welsh and Irish descent, inherited the house in which they lived and which had been in her family for fifty years, when her father died. Thus rents from the other apartments were added to the family income. 'Actually, it was a series of flats, with a common toilet on each floor, out in the hall,' Burt remembered. 'Like our neighbours, we Lancasters just squeaked by. My mother used to say to us boys and my sister, "If you want to know about love, stay in the house. If you want to know about life, go out in the streets." '

On the streets of New York, Lancaster remembered, 'You learn reality young, and it has many faces.' Burt, who topped out at six-foot-two and 185 pounds, was 'a short pudgy boy', according to his sister Jane. 'When he graduated from P.S. 83 at age eleven-and-a-half he was the shortest fellow in his class.' Because of his small size, by the age of eight Burton was the target of local bullies and had already learned two-fisted fighting in self-defence. 'He was a scrapper, all right,' said Jane,

[8]

'he'd fight anyone for a principle and he usually came out on top.'

'Out in the streets, fighting to assert myself at an early age,' said Lancaster, 'made me tough and it made me want to win. But I also had a lot of love and affection. It was a warm neighbourhood. The life of the streets had a warmth in my childhood. My Dad had an old guitar, and on summer nights he'd sit out on the steps and sing in his clear Irish voice. The Italians would listen and applaud Dad. One night I joined in the singing. He dropped out, just playing the accompaniment. That way I rated the applause. It was my first applause. I thoroughly enjoyed it.'

Burt had actually made his stage debut at the age of three, in a church Nativity play. He was supposed to have been strictly an 'atmosphere' player, dressed as a little shepherd, with no lines to speak. It was to be his only work as an extra. On stage little Burton got bored with the pageant and began examining his costume, particularly the chewing gum stuck to his shoe. He began to speculate out loud on how the gum got there, in his earliest unprintable street language. It so startled the congregation that the performance ended early.

Lancaster wouldn't be that outstanding an actor again until he was eleven, but his father James recalled, in a *Photoplay* article in 1953, that his youngest son 'always has been a dreamer. When he was a little kid he could be off in his own dream world for hours, and he wouldn't hear a thing you'd say to him. He was a movie fan, and at seven his great idol was Douglas Fairbanks [Snr]. When *The Mark of Zorro* played the Atlas Theatre in our neighbourhood, Burt was there when the doors opened at 11 a.m. He was still there at 11 that night, forgetting all about lunch and dinner. Naturally his mother was in a tizzy. He'd go around the house jumping over everything in sight, trying to imitate Fairbanks' feats. It never occurred to me that he'd eventually become an athlete; we figured he was going to be the runt of the family. Suddenly, at thirteen, he seemed to begin shooting up overnight, and turned out to be the tallest of the boys.'

The biggest influence on Burt's early life, outside of his family and Fairbanks, was the Union Settlement House on East 104th Street, just two blocks from where he lived. 'Our settlement house, a sort of youth club and sports centre, was one of the biggest,' he recalled. 'You could play basketball, do gymnastics, study art, learn languages and act in plays.' Lancaster did some of each, even though he said he considered acting 'sissy stuff. But I did it because I got "plus marks"; when you got enough plus marks you would be sent off to summer camp. For a kid from East Harlem in the early 1920s to go to summer camp was really something. You looked forward to it all year. That meant more than anything.'

At camp the summer he was nine, Burt became friends with Nick Cravat, an Italian-American boy from East 108th Street. They shared each other's fights and began practising hand balancing acrobatics. Back in New York City at the end of the summer, they became inseparable at P.S. 83 and the Union Settlement House. 'Nick Cravat was my best friend,' Lancaster said of the man who remained so and worked with Burt as an acrobat and in several movies. 'Nick's mother was a coat-maker who spent her life lighting candles for his soul. At eighteen he'd already had sixteen professional fights. We called him "Little Dempsey". He weighed only 126 pounds but he could sink his fist into a lath-and-plaster wall.'

Risking his friends' scorn and somewhat countering

his own self-image, Lancaster worked many years as an amateur in reproductions of Broadway plays at the settlement house. 'I was very fortunate, because at the time there was a professional group in New York called the American Laboratory Theatre. Its director was Richard Boleslawski and part of the training was to send people to the various settlement houses in poorer sections of the city, and have them teach and direct amateur performances. So I did have something of a background when I went into the theatre and then into films.' The Polish-born Boleslawski, who did not work with Lancaster directly (his students did), had been at the Moscow Art Theatre when Stanislavsky's theories were instituted. Boleslawski later, in the 1930s, directed Hollywood movies: *Rasputin and the Empress* with the Barrymores, *The Painted Veil* with Greta Garbo, *The Garden of Allah* with Charles Boyer and Marlene Dietrich, and *Les Miserables* with Fredric March and Charles Laughton.

Lancaster kept this once-removed, semi-distinguished acting background a secret well into later life, however, and deliberately let his first chance to take the 'sissy stuff' beyond the settlement house slip by. A play by Booth Tarkington entitled *Three Pills in a Bottle*, in which he appeared when he was eleven, could have proved the turning point in Lancaster's life had he let it. 'I played a little boy in a wheelchair who was dying from leukaemia or something, and taught everyone the meaning of love,' he remembered. Two talent scouts saw his performance and visited the Lancaster apartment to ask Burt's mother if he could study on an acting scholarship. He hid out on the fire-escape until the men went away. His mother knew he was there but did not betray him.

Burt recalled his mother, who died when he was

sixteen, as 'a strong-willed, formidable character who insisted on honesty, truth and loyalty. One day my mother gave me a quarter to go for a quart of milk. They'd pour it in a pail, and charge seven or eight cents. It was hot that day, and on the way home I couldn't resist taking a drink, although I knew Mom would give me the back of her hand for doing it. But the milk was wonderful, and I thought it would be worth it. I got a licking all right, but not for that. I got it because I hadn't noticed that the man had given me five cents too much in change. After the whipping she sent me back with the nickel. A couple of years later I found a twenty-dollar bill in a bank. I stood for almost half an hour, hoping nobody would claim it. It looked like the riches of Midas to me. Why, I'd never even had a whole dollar I could call my own. Finally, an agitated old woman rushed in looking for the bill. It broke my heart, but Mom's lesson stuck with me. I handed it over.'

While his father James was 'a kind, gentle, warm sort of man, Mom was like a little dictator with us kids, and lots of times she was wrong,' Lancaster said. 'But she was honest and strong in her own lights, and she gave me an understanding of the real values of life. She was a woman with a great capacity for love, but also a woman who had great strength. She brought me up to believe that a man's word is his bond, that he should honour a promise. I suppose I never really forgot it. She was the one who made the decisions and did the punishing. When I first became a father I was very strict, too. Then I began to realise that children are individuals with minds of their own and that I must have looked pretty ridiculous being so firm all the time. So I learned to let them alone. I became convinced that what they really respect is the example I set for them.'

Lancaster inherited his mother's temper, but not her tact. 'Bums were forever knocking at our door for a handout', he remembered. 'First my mother would bawl them out, then she'd feed them. And what tact she had: she used to talk broken English to the neighbours, because *they* talked broken English.'

When Burt was twelve, a policeman dragged him home by the scruff of his neck. Burt had had trouble with a storekeeper in the neighbourhood and had responded to the policeman's interest in the situation by throwing beer bottles off a warehouse roof. 'It's a fair question I ask ye,' said the officer, like virtually all other New York City cops in those days an Irish-American, to James Lancaster. 'Do you keep your kid off the streets or do we?'

But there was no keeping Burt off the streets. 'We boys had the run of all New York,' he recalled. 'Sure we ran in gangs, but we fought only with our fists or stones and sticks, although some of the kids on our block carried knives.'

Burt's pranks were pretty tame compared to those of some of his neighbours, and certainly compared to many arrested in East Harlem later in the century. Vincent Franzone, a boyhood chum who continued to live on the Lancaster's street as an adult and became a dental technician, recalled: 'Burt and I and a fellow we called Moby Dick ran together. We used to swim off 104th Street. There was an old gravel barge there, and we'd dive in and swim across to Ward's Island, a quarter of a mile away. On the way home, wet and dripping, we'd pass through the old farmers' market. Once in a while, we'd swipe a couple of apples from the pushcarts, and the peddlars would give us a good run home.'

Playing 'stickball' and 'stoopball' on the busy streets of East Harlem, particularly Third Avenue, Burt was hit by automobiles eight times. So he switched to the Union Settlement House's indoor baseball field, and Central Park just five blocks away, where there were 'tremendous baseball fields and play areas. Besides all that, there were backyards and roofs to play on, and four schools that kept their recreational facilities open in the evening.' More than he cared to admit to his cronies, Burt also made use of the Settlement House music room (he took piano lessons) and its art classes, as well as the local branch of the New York Public Library, on 110th Street. 'I imagined myself as a character in every book I read,' Lancaster recalled.

Burton also sang (soprano) in the church choir until he was fifteen. 'Then my voice broke,' he remembered, 'and I spent the rest of my life searching for it.' His first ambition was to be an opera singer, and he used to sing John McCormack songs for Italian mothers in the neighbourhood, who would reward him with cake and milk. He listened to Lily Pons and Giuseppe di Luca on the radio, and saw at least half of many performances at the Metropolitan Opera downtown. 'My neighbourhood was full of opera singers, amateur and professional,' Lancaster recalled. 'Somehow it wasn't considered sissy to try to sneak into the opera house with people who had actually paid to get in. We all did it. I don't think I ever paid for a ticket. I'd stand outside until the interval, then walk in, and invariably I'd find a seat.'

Lancaster, in looking back on his childhood, never expressed any sense of deprivation. 'My background was potluck, and everybody had to share,' he acknowledged. 'I wore my brothers' hand-me-down clothes, but when you're that young that just doesn't matter. You expected not to be quite warm enough in the winter. So you ran and ran to keep warm. I was lucky.

We weren't poor in the sense that we were starving. We had all the food we needed on the table. In those days food was cheap. My mother would send me to the corner store and I'd get all the greens thrown in for nothing. At the butcher shop all the sweetbreads and hearts were given to you. We didn't lack for anything. My mother always said to us, "You are your own slum area. You can make it as mean or as meaningful as you wish." '

As a teenager, Lancaster had both meaningful and mean moments. 'At fourteen I learned my first respect for stern Jewish morality,' he remembered, 'because I had fallen in love with a Jewish girl. I first knew there was something called Art from David Morrison, who taught at the Union Settlement House. When I was growing up, people in East Harlem helped each other, it was a community, people cared, took pride in the kids who got on, like my brothers who went to New York University.'

But, assigned one evening to 'locker room duty' at the Settlement, Burt was visited by two fifteen-year-old boys, who apparently had a right to be in the facility. 'Get out of here,' Lancaster ordered, feeling the authority of a boy a year or two older, 'you're getting in my hair.' The two youths refused to move, and heated words were exchanged, then punches. Burt got one of the boys on the floor and the other was halfway out the door, when suddenly one of them produced a pocket knife. Burt punched, but missed, and the knife shot out, catching him in the hip. The two boys fled. Lancaster was released three days later from Lennox Hill Hospital. 'That little incident did Burt in,' recalled Helen Harris, then a director of the Settlement House. 'Those were tough years in East Harlem. The

Depression was in full swing, and a major revolt was going on inside of every boy – including Burt.'

Once he achieved his full growth, Lancaster developed some skill in basketball, and when he graduated from DeWitt Clinton High School in 1930, at age sixteen, he accepted a basketball scholarship to New York University, a private school 'downtown', where his elder brother Jim became captain of the basketball team. At DeWitt Clinton, where he had neither excelled nor done poorly in his studies, Burt had concentrated his interest on literature and drama. But at NYU he pursued a programme aimed towards his becoming a physical education instructor. While at the university, Burt also continued to coach basketball at the Union Settlement House. 'Burt showed lots of promise as an athlete,' said Ben Puleo, who was best man at James Lancaster, Jnr's wedding and coached Burt in basketball at the Central Jewish Institute. 'At eighteen he was slim and muscular. He could have been a really good basketball player if he had stuck with the game.'

Curly Brent eliminated that possibility. Charles 'Curly' Brent was an Australian gymnast who one day happened to be rehearsing giant swings on a bar at the Union Settlement House when Burt walked by in the summer between his graduation from DeWitt Clinton and his entrance to NYU. Lancaster and Nick Cravat were fascinated by Brent's movements, so the Australian began teaching them how to do swings. Then he advanced them into such movements as 'kip-ups' and 'somersaults-away'.

Nick and Burt persuaded the Union Settlement's Helen Harris to let them drill eight holes in the floor of the gymnasium for a second set of horizontal bars, which they would build, even though the gym had just been refurbished at a cost of $1500. 'They came in every day for a week with the same request,' Harris recalled. 'I was getting a sore neck and I couldn't get any work done. Finally I said, "all right – drill the blasted holes".'

Burt installed yet a third set of bars in the backyard of his father's apartment, working out there 'for hours on end', according to his sister Jane. After two years of practise, together and separately, Burt and Nick formed an acrobatic act, Nick abandoning his career as a boxer in the flyweight class. It was the spring of 1932. Lancaster was nineteen, and bored with NYU's lecture hall approach to higher education. He and Nick dubbed themselves 'Lang and Cravat' for brevity in marquee billing, and combed the trade publication *Billboard* for possible bookings. The newspaper said that the Kay Brothers Circus was enroute from its winter quarters in Florida to Petersburg, Virginia, and the pair wrote to the show asking for work. They heard nothing back, so, at the end of his sophomore year at NYU, Burt left school for good. 'We thought we had the act down slick,' he remembered, 'so we paid ninety dollars for a fifth-hand jalopy, and headed south.'

An early publicity still

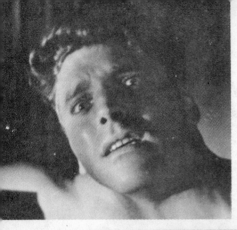

The Killers, 1946

With Lizabeth Scott on the set of *I Walk Alone*, 1947

With Peter Lorre, *Rope of Sand*, 1949

With Dorothy McGuire, *Mr 880*, 1950

As Jim Thorpe, in *Jim Thorpe. All-American*, 1951

Eating lunch with co-star Jody Lawrence on the set of *Ten Tall Men*, 1951

As the alcoholic 'Doc' in *Come Back. Little Sheba*, 1952

With Terry Moore, *Come Back, Little Sheba*, 1952

In a dress as 'Mimi', with Veola (cq) Vonn in *South Sea Woman*, 1953

With son Billy and daughter Susan on the set of *South Sea Woman*, 1953

With Deborah Kerr on the beach in *From Here to Eternity*, 1953

Apache, 1954

CHAPTER TWO

Acrobat

LANCASTER AND CRAVAT arrived in Petersburg, Virginia – with a combined thirty dollars in their pockets – on the night before the Kay Brothers' one-ring circus was set to open. The partners talked their way into an audition for the show's manager. 'Lang' and Cravat wore second-hand green boxing tights and leaped about on their own horizontal bars, which they had brought with them in the car. 'On my first jump-up I didn't get enough swing to carry me across,' Lancaster/Lang recalled. 'I hit my knees and fell down. Of course, I was nervous. I tried it again and my timing was still off. I missed the bar and tore my tights.'

Despite the messy try-out and the fact that even small circuses used a triple bar instead of the one the boys had learned on, Burt and Nick were hired on at three dollars a week plus board. While learning new tricks from the Kay Brothers' older bar performer, the fledgling 'stick actors', as circus gymnasts were called, drove in tent stakes, helped raise the tent itself, and carried circus banners in street parades. At the end of one month Lang and Cravat's combined salary was raised to five dollars a week plus board. The pair stayed with the Kay Brothers for about six months, washing out their own tights each night. One night Nick fell and badly smashed his nose. He returned to New York to recover. Burt stayed on briefly as a solo performer, but quit when he found out that Cravat was not going to be taken back and that circus management planned to work Lancaster into another act.

When Nick's nose healed, Lang and Cravat signed on with an agent, who booked them with carnivals and other small circuses, among them the Cole Brothers and the Gorman Brothers. Besides their horizontal bar act, the boys developed a perch pole act, in which Burt balanced on his hands atop a long pole balanced on Nick's head. During a circus stint in 1935, Lancaster met and fell in love with June Ernst, a fellow performer. 'She was the only woman in America who could do horizontal bar tricks,' he said. 'As far as women were concerned it was pretty much a lost art, and nobody appreciated it.'

Burt and June were married, but continued their separate acrobatic acts. When the touring circus hit Waterbury, Connecticut a few months later, Lang and Cravat left it without June Ernst to return to New York. Lancaster's brief first marriage was over. 'It didn't work out,' was all he would ever say on the subject. 'We never had any fights. We just got tired of each other. It ended in divorce.'

Nick and Burt, after regrouping in New York, went out on the road again, wherever they could get a booking. At one point they even did an act briefly with Burt's former mother-in-law, an accomplished trapeze performer. Eventually the partners worked up to the big time, Ringling Brothers Circus, for $300 a week.

Burt quit the road for a time to try performing with the Federal Theatre Project of the Works Projects Administration. The WPA, established by President Franklin Roosevelt during the Depression, to ease unemployment, was a particular success in its theatrical productions. But Lancaster felt that he personally worked better as an acrobat and with a partner, so he soon rejoined Cravat, reluctantly leaving his beloved New York of the mid-1930's.

'That was the place and that was the time,' he recalled. 'I can remember seeing Lillian Hellman's *The Children's Hour* in 1935. The whole audience stood up to hiss that little girl at the end of the second act. A year later I saw John Gielgud's *Hamlet*. It was the first Shakespeare I'd ever seen. I had a friend who worked in the box office and he gave us tickets in the second balcony. Orson Welles was with the Federal Theatre. There was the Group, the Civic Repertory and Boleslawsky's American Lab theatre.'

While he enjoyed the theatre as a spectator, Lancaster still felt his occupation was acrobat. But he and Cravat, attempting to better their relatively meagre incomes, switched from circuses to vaudeville and nightclubs for a while. They toured for a time on the Poli vaudeville circuit, but for a mere fifteen dollars a week between them. Also, to set up their bar rigging in clubs or on theatre stages meant drilling holes in the floor, which most owners were unwilling to tolerate. And their perch pole specialty was too lofty for most stages. The top man, usually Burt, was hidden behind the proscenium arch, out of sight of the audience. Since it was the bar act or nothing, Lang and Cravat, as they still were, returned to circuses and fairs.

After a total of seven years of moving about with the act, in 1939 Burt became restless, and frustrated by the acrobatic profession's limited financial and artistic potential. He had had the thrill of finally completing his 'first perfect fly-over. I tried it for four years, and for four years I hit the bar with my knuckles until they bled. Then I got it.' He had also invented a folding bar frame to roll out from the wings of a stage, to get around the problem of holes in the floor. It took more than a year to get the frame to work. It was fine for the diminutive Nick Cravat, but Lancaster's 183 pounds would cause the frame to come up from the floor every time he hit the bars.

While in Los Angeles to do their acrobatics at the Orpheum Theatre, Burt made the rounds of motion picture studios by bus and streetcar, more out of curiosity, he said, than out of hope. Casting directors told him that, despite his good looks, they were not interested in anyone without professional acting experience. They were especially not interested in acrobats. 'Finally,' he recalled, 'we got a booking playing a fair at Hammond, Indiana. We went over big and sat around gassing about how we would play New York's Rainbow Room and live the fat life.' It did not quite go as planned: three weeks later, Lancaster and Cravat were playing a burlesque house in Kansas City. 'Nick kept saying, "We can't miss",' Burt remembered. 'But I said, "Look, we are missing. I'm not a kid anymore. I'm twenty-eight. It's time I tried something else".'

Lancaster's decision to quit the act was helped along by an accident during a circus stint in St Louis. He tore his right hand and developed a serious finger infection. A doctor told Burt that unless he stopped performing, the finger would have to be amputated. 'I lit out for Chicago with one suit – the one on my back,' he said, 'and twenty bucks in my kick.' In Chicago, Lancaster stayed with the Smiletas, a circus family. Cravat found a new partner, a woman who later became his wife.

For the next several months, Lancaster held a variety of jobs in Chicago. He got a job as a floorwalker at Marshall Field's department store, in the ladies' lounging apparel department. 'I drew twenty-five dollars a week, and I learned how to con those dames along,' he recalled. Once the Christmas rush was over, however, he was transferred into menswear, selling shirts and ties. 'After a few months I became so bored that I started kidding the customers,' he said. 'One day I caused a mild panic by walking in the aisles on my hands.'

He expected to be fired for his gymnastics, but was not, so Lancaster quit the store to work for a company that supplied refrigeration and steam heat to Chicago's meat-packing plants. The firm operated seventy coolers, and it was Burt's responsibility to adjust each of them twice a day. Pork and veal had to be kept at forty-two degrees Farenheit, beef even colder than that. At least the job took him outside, travelling from plant to plant, but soon his boredom grew even greater.

Lancaster next applied to an organisation that sold community concerts, knowing that they needed an attention-getting salesman to visit civic leaders around the country. 'I was supposed to fix it so Junior Leaguers could sit in concert halls scratching themselves in a genteel and ladylike manner while they listened to Lawrence Tibbett or some other canary popping off onstage,' he told the *Saturday Evening Post*'s Pete Martin in 1948. 'The trick was to sell them a package deal. They'd get two big concert names for their money, but in order to get them they'd have to take three unknowns.'

Burt had inherited a love of music from his mother,

and his education, particularly in classical music, had come from his settlement house piano lessons and all that 'second-acting' at Town Hall. Certainly the 'conning' part of the experience might have helped him to prepare for his roles in *The Rainmaker*, *Elmer Gantry* and *Atlantic City*. But no sooner had Lancaster arrived in New York, in July 1942, to take up the $6000-a-year job with the Concert Bureau of the Columbia Broadcasting System, than he was drafted. 'That ended my culture peddling,' he said. To fill in the four months before he was actually inducted into the army, Lancaster worked as a singing waiter in a nightclub near Union City, New Jersey, across the Hudson River. An elderly Irish tenor wheezed through 'Mother Machree', followed by Burt singing 'Old Man River'. The club's master of ceremonies also insisted that Burt act as his straight man, which proved to be Lancaster's 'first experience talking out loud in front of people'.

Lancaster began his army career at Fort Riley, Kansas, and was assigned to the Special Services Branch of the Fifth Army. 'I tried to get in the Engineers,' he recalled, 'thinking that because of my experience in rigging and circus work I would be qualified, but I didn't make it.' Because of his show business background, such as it was, Burt was asked to write, direct and act in shows for fellow soldiers. In June, 1943 he landed in North Africa with the Fifth Army, then followed it into Sicily, Italy and Austria. 'I never had one heroic moment,' he remembered. 'They made me an entertainer.' Sometimes he would further deprecate his whole World War II career by saying, 'I had a wonderful time touring Europe as a page-turner for a soldier-pianist. We often went up on the lines and did performances during breaks in the firing, but, to be frank, we were never in any real danger.'

Burt seldom used any of his acrobatic skills in army shows. However, one day in Rome, when a buddy wanted to see the Pope and his chances looked slim, Lancaster used an old circus trick to propel his smallish chum over the heads of a huge crowd waiting outside Pius XII's audience chamber, to the front of the line. The friend got his Papal audience and his rosary blessed by Pius.

Most of his three years in the military, Lancaster spent as a private. On several occasions he worked himself up to sergeant, only to be busted back down again for insubordination. A lieutenant who had had three months of college dramatics tried to tell Lancaster how to behave on stage. Burt 'told him to climb the hell out of my hair and leave me alone'. The altercation cost Lancaster a promotion and increased pay. He also had trouble with a captain who thought Burt's desire to appear in the Army show *Stars and Gripes* was a gold-bricking attempt. The captain punished Lancaster by making him a 'truck jockey' whose job was to try to control giant rubber 'doughnut tyres' in heavy mud. Lancaster appeared in *Stars and Gripes* anyway.

Norma Anderson, a pretty New York stenographer for a radio station, was substituting for an ill performer in a USO (United Services Organisation) show, then also touring Italy. 'When she came to Caserta,' Burt recalled, 'she did an act with five other girls – sort of a take-off on the *Three Musketeers*. Norma saw our show once and wanted to meet me. At first, I wasn't in the mood and didn't feel like meeting her. So all we said was "hello". We didn't get acquainted until later, at a dance.'

Norma was a war widow with a one-year-old son. Norma and Lancaster exchanged addresses and life ambitions (both said they wanted to have four

[25]

children). Back in New York after the war, Norma resumed her job with radio producer Ray Knight, on the eleventh floor of the RCA (Radio Corporation of America) building in Rockefeller Center. Shortly after V-J day, Lancaster was sent back to New York on a forty-five-day terminal furlough. Columbia Concerts was interested in having him back but only after his full discharge. 'I was home from Italy only twenty days, and still in uniform,' Burt recalled, 'when I ran into her again. "I'll introduce you to Mr Knight," she told me, "maybe he can help you kick off into civilian life once more." '

In the elevator of the RCA building one afternoon, togged out in new civvies and on the way to take Norma to lunch, Burt was aware of someone looking at him with great interest. As he put it, 'A guy puts the mince pies [a Cockney expression meaning eyes] on me. I don't like the way he's looking at me, and I'm all ready to bust him. But I manage to get out of the elevator without doing it.' The man followed Lancaster off the elevator and asked, 'Are you an actor?' Burt replied, 'Yes, I'm a dumb actor.'

'I was kidding, referring to an expression – dumb actor – that's used in the circus when you do an act and then don't talk. Acrobats are all called "dumb actors".'

The man was Jack Mahlor, an associate of Irving Jacobs, who was producing *A Sound of Hunting* on Broadway. Mahlor thought Lancaster would be 'exactly right physically' for the role of Sergeant Joseph Mooney, the lead in the new Henry Brown play about a group of GI's in war-torn Cassino, Italy who attempt to rescue one of their number caught between German and American lines. Private First Class (still) Lancaster was asked to read for the part. He got it, contingent on his discharge from the service. With the help of an army chaplain, Burt managed to rush his discharge papers through the separation centre seven hours before rehearsals for *A Sound of Hunting* began. Sam Levene co-starred as a soldier thought to be a coward by his colleagues.

A Sound of Hunting tried out for two weeks in Philadelphia before opening on Broadway in November 1945. Lancaster had just turned thirty-two. The play lasted only twenty-three performances despite critical enthusiasm for Levene's and his portrayals. *PM* called Burton Lancaster, as he was billed, 'attractive', and the New York *Journal-American* called him 'the non-com every private prays for'. A sergeant at last, even if only for a short run, Lancaster professed to have felt no nervousness in his professional acting debut: 'I said to myself, "What can happen to me? I can miss a line, but I can't get hurt." ' He did acknowledge that he 'probably never would have made the effort on my own to become an actor, because I never dreamed I was capable of doing something like that'. Burt blamed the failure of the play on its being a bitter war drama, at a time when audiences were sick of the war.

Nonetheless, his own experience on stage convinced Lancaster to forego the security of the concert-booking business and pursue acting full-time. Levene offered to help sift through the several movie offers that resulted from their brief three-week run. 'He told me I'd be hitting the free lunch circuit,' Burt said, 'eating in all the places I never thought I could afford, with somebody else picking up the tab. "Tell you what I'll do," said Levene, "I'll represent you." So Sam would go along and do the talking while I listened. Harold Hecht had started his own agency and was in the east on business. Sam introduced us, and Hecht levelled with me. "I know everybody," he said, "but I have few

[27]

clients. If you sign with me, you'd be important to me. I'd work harder for you, because I want to eat and I'd have to keep you working." That made sense, so I signed.'

Hecht was a former dancer who had worked with Martha Graham, then headed the literary department of the Goldstone Agency. Lancaster found his 'honesty and outspokenness' 'impressive'. Hecht and Lancaster decided, at a dinner the night they agreed to do business, that they really wanted to produce movies. 'Suddenly we began laughing,' Burt remembered. 'Here we were, a couple of bums without a quarter between us, discussing producing our own pictures. Hecht laughed: "You never can tell. Maybe in five years we can make it." '

Hal Wallis, a producer who had recently left Warner Brothers to run his own independent unit at Paramount, was building a stock company of new stars that included Kirk Douglas and Lizabeth Scott. At the suggestion of one of his employees, Wallis saw Lancaster in *A Sound of Hunting*. 'He was excellent as the drill sergeant, a martinet with a striking command and attack,' Wallis recalled. 'Looking at Burt's huge shoulders and big, capable hands, I knew women would be delighted with him. I went backstage, introduced myself, complimented him on his performance and offered him a job in our stock company. Burt was cool and quite unimpressed, suggested that I see his agent to discuss terms, and closed his dressing-room door. I saw his agent, Harold Hecht, and proposed what I thought was a very generous deal: a two-picture-a-year contract, with the right to make other pictures on the side. Burt accepted it as his due.'

Lancaster and Hecht agreed to go with Wallis rather than any other producer because of the option to make pictures for other studios, one a year so long as he did his two for Wallis. But even as Burt and the producer walked to the latter's New York lawyer's office to sign Lancaster's preliminary contract, the actor asserted his no-nonsense independence. As they were walking along Broadway, Wallis pointed to a billboard for a big film due to open. 'I produced that picture,' he said proudly, 'would you like to see it when it opens?'

'I should say not,' replied Lancaster, 'I saw it in Italy. It stinks.'

Like all the other competing offers, Wallis's was predicated on Burt's taking and passing a screentest in Hollywood. 'My deal was $100 a week for four weeks and a first-class train ticket to the coast and back,' Lancaster remembered. 'If Wallis hadn't liked the test I would have been back in New York. Nowhere.'

As it turned out, both Lancaster and *A Sound of Hunting* made it in Hollywood, the latter as the movie *Eight Iron Men* in 1952, with Lee Marvin in Burt's old role. Lancaster's own success came a great deal faster than that.

CHAPTER THREE

Hollywood

L<small>ANCASTER ARRIVED IN</small> Hollywood for his Hal Wallis screentest in January 1946, two months past his thirty-second birthday. He wore a pair of borrowed shoes, and carried thirty dollars in cash. While changing trains in Chicago, Burt had sent both his suits to be cleaned and pressed, but the tailor was late in returning them. To avoid missing his California train, Lancaster left the suits and travelled in shirt and slacks, a bit casual for 1946. Harold Hecht's first act as Burt's welcoming agent was to borrow a leather jacket for him from Robert Preston. Like most New Yorkers, Lancaster had assumed that California was warm, even on a winter night. Wallis turned Burt over to Byron Haskin, a Wallis staff director, headquartered with the rest of the company on the Paramount lot. Burt arrived at Haskin's office as Haskin was reading a script, and asked, with characteristic brusqueness, 'You Haskin?'

'Yes, I'm Byron Haskin,' came the reply.

'My name's Lancaster, Burt Lancaster.'

'Oh?'

'Yeah. I'm supposed to read for you.'

'Yes?'

'Yeah?'

'Well, I've no objection, Mr Lancaster.'

Lancaster started rearranging the furniture in Haskin's office to resemble the frontline trench under enemy siege in *A Sound of Hunting*. He began a scene from the play, recreating his hard-swearing, fighting GI. From surrounding offices, producers, writers, secretaries and office boys rushed to Haskin's room to see what all the noise was about. In his Hollywood debut, Lancaster was suddenly playing to a full house. Haskin and the rest of the audience were sufficiently impressed for Haskin to arrange the screentest. Burt was to get the previously agreed-upon $100 a week while preparing for the test, which would take about a month; a flat fee of $10,000 if he passed it; and $1250 weekly for the next seven years while working in movies for Wallis, or on loan-out.

The test was 'a scene from the film that would be called *Desert Fury*, although at the time I didn't know what it came from,' Lancaster recalled. He passed the screentest, but *Desert Fury*, which was to have been his first film for Wallis, was not scheduled to begin shooting until August. Lancaster was just about to use the other half of his round-trip train ticket to return to New York for a while, when he heard of a project that Mark Hellinger was preparing at Universal. Hellinger, for whom one of Broadway's major legitimate musical theatres is named, had begun as a New York newspaperman, moved to Hollywood to write scripts, and produced several movies for Warner Brothers before setting up his own company at Universal. *The Killers*, Hemingway's sixteen-page short story, had been acquired by Hellinger as his first independent production.

Anthony Veiller was hired to expand the Hemingway story into a screenplay. The important casting was 'The Swede', a dumb former boxer who gets involved with criminals and a bad-but-beautiful girl, who is the story's victim. Hellinger wanted Wayne Morris from Warner Brothers, but that studio asked $75,000 for the loan-out, way beyond Hellinger's budget. Universal, on the other hand, was insisting on a 'name' male actor. Sonny Tufts was considered, then rejected as lacking sufficient talent for the complex part. Lancaster knew of these deliberations and the availability of the role. He got a member of Wallis's staff, Marty Juroc, who had once worked for Hellinger, to sneak the Lancaster screentest to Hellinger at Universal. Hellinger was interested enough to arrange a meeting with the new and yet untried movie actor.

'I had always been a Hemingway afficionado,' Lancaster allowed. 'I'd read everything he'd ever written.' In his meeting with Hellinger, Lancaster deliberately downplayed his own personality, acted awkward and loutish, in effect giving Hellinger an audition for the part of the Swede. Hellinger recalled of that first meeting: 'This guy was big, really big. His hair was tousled. No tie. And his suit looked as if it hadn't been pressed since C. Aubrey Smith [an elderly silent movie character actor] was in short pants. But there was something about him. All the time I was talking to him, that smart guy was playing the dumb Swede for me. The Swede I had in mind was big, dumb, awkward and fumbling. The day I met him Lancaster was all four. When you get to know him you realise he's anything but the last three.'

The producer, who was later to refer to Burt as 'the

big, brawny bird', nevertheless subjected him to another screentest. Hellinger asked Lancaster what he thought of *The Killers* script. 'I said, "Well, the first sixteen pages are pure Hemingway verbatim, and after that you have a rather interesting whodunnit film, but nothing comparable to Hemingway," ' Burt remembered. 'He said, "Well you're not really a dumb Swede after all." And I said I didn't think I was.'

Lancaster got the part, and Ava Gardner, in her first major serious role, was cast as his girlfriend. The story is told in flashbacks, from the night that two men (Charles McGraw and William Conrad) arrive in a small town with a contract to kill the Swede. Through the device of an insurance investigator (Edmond O'Brien), *The Killers* explains how the Swede's life deteriorated to this point, and how he was double-crossed both by the crooks and the tramp. Robert Siodmak, perhaps best known as the director of *The Spiral Staircase*, was 'particularly well fitted to directing it', felt Burt. 'He was a charming, engaging man but strong dramatic films were his metier. He was a graduate of the old UFA school – very inventive with the camera. We started in April and finished in eight weeks.'

The Killers was quickly readied for distribution in August 1946. To launch his new contract player, albeit in someone else's movie, Wallis planned to change Burt's name to Stuart Chase. It was pointed out to the producer that Stuart Chase was the name of a famous living economist, who might object. Hellinger and Wallis tried to come up with something better, Burton Lancaster being considered a bit too long for the marquee – a tradition that went back at least to Kathleen Morrison's becoming Colleen Moore. One morning Hellinger telephoned Wallis to say, somewhat excitedly, that his secretary Myrtle 'suggests we use

Burt's real name'. Wallis went along. 'It's amazing what Hollywood brains can accomplish if they give it the works,' Hellinger later cracked.

The picture turned out to be one of the significant hits of 1946, elevating both Lancaster and Ava Gardner to stardom, and establishing Hellinger as a major producer. *The Killers* remains a classic of *film noir*, faithful to Hemingway or not, and it began a vogue for American movies about dumb but fundamentally decent men done in by 'wrong' women. Lancaster himself would star in a few more of them. During the making of the movie, according to columnist Sheilah Graham, Burt had been so unsure of himself that Siodmak would sometimes have to shoot fifteen takes of one small scene, embarrassing Lancaster, who 'apologised humbly'. But no such lack of self-assurance showed on screen in *The Killers*, or in fact was ever to surface again. The New York *Herald-Tribune*'s Otis Guernsey, Jnr wrote of Burt: 'He portrays a likeable fall guy in a most promising screen debut.'

Lancaster himself felt grateful for the accidental vehicle in which he made his movie bow. 'In *The Killers* I was a big, dumb Swede,' he said. 'I could be very simple in the part; there was no need to be highly ostentatious or theatrical. For a new actor this is much easier than something histrionic. There's no question about the good fortune of being ushered into films in that kind of role.'

The success of the movie also made him glad all over again that he and Hecht had had the foresight to insist on outside options, or he could not have done *The Killers* at all. Hellinger signed Lancaster to a second contract, to take advantage of two more Wallis loan-outs, to do *Brute Force* and a second – as yet undesignated – picture beyond that.

[35]

But first he had to do his two pictures for Wallis. 'The part I was to play in *Desert Fury* was a good one,' he recalled, 'but very definitely a secondary kind of role. If I had done it before *The Killers*, it's impossible to say how long it would have been before I'd have been given anything that would have captured the public's fancy. Hal Wallis re-wrote all of *Desert Fury* to enlarge my role because he suddenly decided he had a star on his hands.'

The new star, Hollywood's first emergent male lead since World War II, was nearly thirty-three and genuinely that rarest sort of success: an 'overnight' one. Lancaster's long apprenticeship – he was a bit old to be a beginner at anything – had been served in the army, circuses and life, in what people of that generation called 'the school of hard knocks'. But he certainly hadn't suffered years of hard work in films, or repeated disappointments in his attempts to reach the top of the movie star profession.

'A great case can be made here for luck,' he acknowledged, 'but it was one of those instances of being the right actor in the right spot at the right time. It might not have happened had I been just another movie actor who had played bits. That way an actor tends to come to attention rather slowly. If you're in an important Broadway play, you have a better chance because it's the proper showcase. If you're in a play and have a good role and you're exciting in it, and if you have the physical equipment that is important to motion pictures – how you look, how you move – you are more apt to get a break that way. And when you do come to Hollywood, you come under more important circumstances. In my case it was very much a matter of being in good physical condition. Movies are, in a large sense, a matter of movement and physical excite-

[36]

ment, and you can get by if you move well and have a certain physical presence. Good condition helps in any kind of acting.'

Just after *The Killers* was released, *Desert Fury* was finally put into production, with Lancaster's role expanded. It was shot in Technicolor, a rare occurrence in 1946-47, and had a musical score by Miklos Rozsa that was more dramatic than the screenplay. Wallis paired his new hot property with another member of his contractee class of 1946, Lizabeth Scott. Scott played the spoiled but refined daughter of wealthy brothel-casino owner (Mary Astor) in a desert gambling town. Lancaster co-starred – despite the script re-write and star billing, his role was still secondary – as a somewhat shy local law enforcement officer who loves Scott but cannot have her until the killer-crook (John Hodiak) with whom she is infatuated has been exposed and eliminated. Wendell Corey, another actor whom Wallis had found on his recent foray to Broadway, made his movie debut as Hodiak's sidekick. Wallis recalled asking Lancaster, on the set of *Desert Fury*, how he was getting along. 'Okay, I guess,' came the somewhat cold, offhand reply, 'but I won't be doing this much longer. I'll soon be directing.'

Lancaster's second picture for Wallis in 1947 turned out to be a simple matter for both the player and his producer. (Wallis was not at all unhappy to make much of his money renting his stable out to other producers, so long as he continued to control the contract, and paid the actor only his weekly salary, keeping the often considerable overage for himself; this was common practice both among big studios and independent producers up until the early 1960s.) Paramount, which distributed all of Wallis's pictures at the time, was producing an all-star musical, *Variety Girl*. Literally dozens of Paramount stars and contract featured performers appeared in the behind-the-scenes Hollywood extravaganza, which was also generous with its scenes of the Paramount lot. Burt was again teamed with Lizabeth Scott, he as a cowboy who shoots a cigarette out of her mouth. In the blackout sketch he fires the shot, and a puff of smoke appears. The scene then cuts to Lancaster setting up a sign saying 'Girl Wanted'.

Brute Force, Hellinger's realistic prison drama, was to prove Lancaster's consolidation as an original screen presence. He was top-billed as Joe Collins, one of five inmates whose unfortunate stories are told, largely in flashback, as the *film noir* unfolds. The flashbacks had the dual purpose of relieving the prison setting, and bringing pretty women into the picture. Burt's part had him obsessed with escaping from jail in order to be with his girlfriend (Ann Blyth) while she has a cancer operation – which she refuses to undergo unless he is there. The screenplay, his first, was written by Richard Brooks (based on the story by Robert Patterson).

Brooks had written his first book, *The Brick Foxhole*, during the war, when he has in the Marine Corps. Hellinger had read it and written to Brooks; 'If you ever get out alive, and discharged, come and see me.' Brooks did, first working on the *The Killers*. It was during *Brute Force* in 1947 that Brooks first spoke to Lancaster about his desire to do a movie version of Sinclair Lewis's novel *Elmer Gantry*.

Jules Dassin, still several years prior to his exile from Hollywood for left-wing political sympathies, was hired to direct *Brute Force*. Producer, director, writer and star were united in their desire to portray the complex criminal characters, their feelings of futility and hatred, and the conditions under which they were incarcerated

[38]

– rather than just telling an adventure story. The end result was more realism than most movie-goers of 1947 were accustomed to in a Hollywood movie (though less than the norm for later decades). The Collins/Lancaster character does organise a prison break, but in the attempt he and all of his cronies are killed. Burt was credited with a 'brooding, effective performance' by the New York *Herald-Tribune*, despite 'Dassin's great many close-ups of Lancaster looking steely-eyed and unshaven'.

'A good film,' *Brute Force* remained one of Lancaster's favourites. 'It was very potent,' he added, 'and I think for those particular days it was a larger-than-life approach to things. The characters were all very strong, and very romantically written as opposed to the documentary approach to that kind of film.'

He admitted that Universal's insistence on casting four of its most appealing female newcomers (Blyth, Anita Colby, Yvonne De Carlo and Ella Raines) for added box office allure may have been a bit gratuitous, if typical for the late 1940s. (A photograph of De Carlo was used in the movie's advertising, accompanied by the copy: 'This kind of woman drives men to prison – and then drives them crazy to get out.')

'This was all part of Hollywood then,' Lancaster defended. 'The emphasis was always with the love story. A film could be about Gable or Tracy, but the conflict was always with a woman who loved Gable or Tracy. The feeling was that people always wanted to see some sort of love story; and the truth is that this still prevails today in the so-called popular film. Or even, in a deeper sense, we often say that no story's worth telling unless it's a love story. We don't mean that it has to be a boy-girl or man-woman love story. It can be something about the love of an idea or a cause, or the hatred of an establishment, which means therefore the love of humanity. But in those days they made films for very safe reasons. They believed that what was known to work well at the box office should not be tampered with. So in *Brute Force* the men in jail had to have love interests on the outside, to create a sympathetic link. If one of the girls didn't really love the man but was just using him, that made you feel sorry for him – and so on.'

Lancaster referred to Dassin as 'extraordinary' and 'a very fine director', although Sheilah Graham reported that during production Burt 'was already telling the director how to direct'. Nonetheless, Lancaster acknowledged that with Dassin, 'I could see that I was working with a man who was knowledgeable and helpful, someone who could excite new ideas in terms of how you wanted to play the part.'

Burt also saw his role as a step toward social commentary, and a distinct advance from 'The Swede' in *The Killers*. 'The Swede was confused and lacked sophistication,' he said, 'so when his love affair with the glamorous Ava Gardner went to pieces, he literally didn't care to live anymore, which is some indication of his limits, if you like. But for Collins in *Brute Force* it was another matter. He wasn't stupid. Of course he had a sticky, sentimental relationship with Ann Blyth; he loved her dearly, and under examination that was a very weak situation really. But there was one prevailing thing: Collins, in his own uneducated way, was a strong and shrewd man with a growing desire to be free. No prison should hold anybody – that's the way he felt. It's a concept that was thought of as romantic in those days, but now we recognise the fallibility of the penal system, and its inability to do any good. Societies are at last having to face the idea that just putting people in jail doesn't do any good anymore, and that maybe society itself has to come up with a new concept of how to deal with people who break its laws.'

By the end of his first two years in movies, Lancaster had strong opinions about his experiences so far in Hollywood, and he had begun his career-long obsession with the quality of stories. Mark Hellinger, who died suddenly of a heart attack at the age of forty-four, shortly after the completion of *Brute Force*, was Burt's first Hollywood hero. Hal Wallis, the holder of the Lancaster seven-year contract, was anything but. 'Hellinger was a much more capable man than Wallis in dealing with stories of literary quality,' Lancaster recalled. 'Wallis surely didn't like to spend money. His name is on *Casablanca* and some others. But that was because he was an executive producer at Warner Brothers. He had nothing to do with the pictures, nothing to speak of, nothing creative. When he became his own producer, he set out to make money. He knew how to make a picture on a slim budget that managed to have some shine to it. But Hellinger was something else. He was going to put me in a story he was planning about a robbery similar to the Brinks hold-up. Ours was going to be job at the Hollywood race-track, an involved thing going into technical and personal aspects of a planned crime. A group of six or eight guys would pull a complicated job in spite of all sorts of odds against them, and protective measures by the police. Hellinger had notes on it, but he died before he could put it into shape.'

Lancaster's only other frustration towards the end of 1947 seemed to be financial. He said to Hellinger, shortly before the producer's death, 'You know, Mark, I don't seem to have any money.'

[41]

The producer replied, 'Well, you won't. You'll owe the government a great deal of money, you'll be broke for a long while.'

'But I don't see how,' said Bert, 'I lead a fairly moderate life.'

'You have your father out here,' explained Hellinger, 'you have your brother [James] out as your lawyer. You've just bought a car for your brother and one for yourself, and you've just bought a house and so forth. Well, if you keep that up, you're going to be broke – in trouble.'

'I thought about it quite seriously,' Lancaster remembered, 'and decided that the only responsibility and obligation I had was to try to do my work well and not worry about those areas in which I am not the wisest man. And the moment I stopped thinking or worrying about finances I found myself in the black. I began to worry only about my work.'

CHAPTER FOUR

Producer

IT TOOK KIRK DOUGLAS a few years longer than Lancaster to become a star, although he was brought to Hollywood by Wallis in the same 1946 wave as Burt, and from the same source: Broadway. Douglas had made an indelible impression opposite Barbara Stanwyck in *The Strange Love of Martha Ivers* in 1947, but it wasn't until his unforgettable male lead in Joseph L. Mankiewicz's *A Letter to Three Wives* the following year, and, even more so, after *Champion* in 1949, that Kirk approached Lancaster in box office appeal and potency. But before all that, Wallis decided to team his two young male Broadway discoveries in *I Walk Alone*, for release early in 1948. Wallis added Lizabeth Scott (in her third and last picture with Lancaster) and Wendell Corey from his stock company.

The movie itself didn't do much of anything for its principals except to encourage the beginning of one of Hollywood's most durable friendships and intermittent acting teams: Kirk Douglas and Burt Lancaster. In addition to their thirty-eight-year personal relationship ('love-hate' is how Douglas described it, only half kidding), Burt and Kirk co-starred in six films together, including the classic western *Gunfight at the OK Corral*, *Seven Days in May* and the television movie *Victory at Entebbe*. They also starred together on stage as Tom Sawyer (Douglas) and Huckleberry Finn (Lancaster) at the ages of sixty, in 1981's *The Boys of Autumn* in San Francisco.

'That's where our friendship began,' recalled Lancaster of *I Walk Alone*. 'We both came from sort of, well, shall we say, humble beginnings. We were both young, brash, cocky, arrogant. We knew everything, were highly opinionated. We were invincible. Nobody liked us.'

That first Douglas-Lancaster collaboration, however, was strictly a pot-boiler, based on a Broadway flop, *Beggars are Coming to Town*. Directed by Byron Haskin, who had first tested Burt, *I Walk Alone* was similar to *The Killers* only in that it had Lancaster as one of two ex-rum runners released from prison after fourteen years for a crime he didn't commit. He seeks revenge on his accomplice (Douglas) who framed him and avoided prison himself. Douglas is now a smooth racketeer working out of a swanky nightclub, and in the process of trying to get even with him, Lancaster's character falls for the club's 'chick singer' (Scott), who is also Douglas's girlfriend. The movie's promotional blurb summed it up thus: 'If you want to pump a guy, send for a dame.' The modestly-budgeted movie made some money, but also brought Burt his first really bad reviews. Bosley Crowther, in *The New York Times*, wrote that Lancaster's portrayal had 'the blank-faced aplomb of Tarzan'. Lancaster himself said *I Walk Alone* and his first Wallis picture, *Desert Fury*, 'can only be described as lightweight in their value'.

[44]

To reverse this situation, Lancaster willingly suffered a large salary cut to play the second lead to Edward G. Robinson in *All My Sons*, Universal's movie version of Arthur Miller's play indicting war profiteering. The play, as directed by Elia Kazan, had won the New York Drama Critics Circle Award as Best Play in 1947, and run a respectable nine months on Broadway. Wallis was opposed to this particular loan-out for Lancaster largely for prestige reasons: neither the subject matter nor the second billing to Robinson was calculated to do anything for Wallis or his investment/protégé, he felt. But Burt fought and pleaded with Wallis for the chance to play, for the first time, a truly decent man. 'I had seen the Arthur Miller play on Broadway and was anxious to get this role,' he remembered. 'I believed in the material and was convinced that it belonged on the screen.'

The story of *All My Sons* centres on Robinson, a manufacturer who knowingly sells defective airplane parts to the government because his business is in trouble and he needs the money to support his wife (Mady Christians) and children. The faulty parts result in the deaths of twenty-one airmen – one of whom is Robinson's own son. Robinson stands trial for the sale of the defective parts, but only his partner (Frank Conroy) goes to jail. A second son (Lancaster) returns from the service, embittered but in love with Conroy's daughter (Louisa Horton). Visiting the partner in jail, Lancaster learns the truth about his father's involvement and tries to make Robinson see what he has done. He finds a letter from his dead brother saying that he knowingly went to his death in suicidal retribution for their father's role in the previous deaths of his comrades. This revelation prompts Robinson's own suicide.

Perhaps understandably, given the subject matter, *All My Sons* was not a box office success. The critics were only half kind. The New York *Herald-Tribune*'s Howard Barnes wrote; 'While there are scenes of fine indignation . . . realised to the full by Edward G. Robinson, Burt Lancaster, Mady Christians and Frank Conroy, they do not offset fabricated situations and blurred characterisations.'

To Lancaster, none of that mattered. Of his role as Chris Keller he said, 'I wanted to play him because he had the courage to make his father realise that he was just as responsible for the deaths of many servicemen as if he had murdered them. And, as I had been in the army, I had no difficulty in duplicating Chris's feelings. I believe that each person shares a responsibility for the welfare of others.' If nothing else, *All My Sons* gave Hollywood its first exposure to Lancaster as an outspoken philosophical, if not yet political, personality.

Having made his radio debut, along with Kirk Douglas and Lizabeth Scott, on May 24 1948, in a live broadcast of *I Walk Alone* on the 'Lux Radio Theatre', Lancaster and Robinson repeated their *All My Sons* parts on NBC radio's 'Camel Screen Guild Players' in November of that year. In his autobiography, *All My Yesterdays*, Robinson wrote that during the making of *All My Sons* there was no need to infuse Lancaster with any enthusiasm for the enterprise. He was already 'showing that animal vitality and suppressed volcano inside that inevitably made him a star'.

By mid-1948, Lancaster was a movie star who received or at least commanded a price-tag of $200,000 per picture, an impressive sum at the time. Much of the actual money, of course, went to Wallis, still the holder of Burt's seven-year contract. Nonetheless, both men could take considerable satisfaction in the fact that

Lancaster's name on a movie marquee meant an additional million dollars in box office receipts for a given motion picture – even if he was in a supporting role – again a considerable amount for the period.

Burt and Norma had a second son on 17 November 1947, William Henry, named for Lancaster's late eldest brother. The growing family moved from Malibu to a modest house they bought in Bel-Air, which gave the two boys more room to play, and better befit a big-time 1940s movie star. Burt also bought several unimproved building lots surrounding his home, which would become crucial to his expanding family's increasingly expansive lifestyle. In most other respects, however, Lancaster refused to play the Hollywood game. Nick Cravat was still working for Burt as his trainer three days a week; they practised 'flyovers' on the double horizontal bars. The difference was that they no longer wore made-over tights.

Artistically, too, Lancaster was able to demand and get the best fitting material. Wallis had bought the film rights to Lucille Fletcher's twenty-two minute, virtually one-character, radio play, *Sorry, Wrong Number*, which was given eight major airings between 1943 and 1947. Agnes Moorehead had triumphed with her radio performance as the wealthy hypochondriac who, in effect, buys a good-looking but no-good younger husband. But Wallis did not consider Moorehead enough of a movie name to cast her in the screen part, which then went to Barbara Stanwyck. Fletcher, in adapting her own screenplay, beefed up the part of the husband who schemes to have his wife killed to pay off his gambling debts. But it could still never be more than a supporting role to the female star, a self-styled invalid who spends most of her time in bed on the

[47]

telephone and manages to overhear accidentally the plot to do her in.

'I prevailed upon Hal Wallis to put me into *Sorry, Wrong Number*,' Burt recalled. 'I was out fishing with him one day and we got talking about the film, which of its kind was rather good. The part I played was originally intended, as Wallis explained to me, for someone like actor Lee Bowman, who tended to play characters who were rather weak. But Bowman himself was not going to be in it. They were searching for someone. I said, "Why don't you let me play it?" And Wallis said, "You're too strong for it." Those were his exact words. And I said, "But that's the whole point: a strong-looking boy on the threshold of life allows a woman to buy him and then suffers for it, and all of his character has been drained out of him. And at the beginning of the film they'll believe I'm strong, and the contrast will make for real dramatic excitement." He talked about it to Anatole Litvak, who was to direct it, and Litvak liked the idea.'

Stanwyck still stole the picture, since most of its length focuses on her attempts to stay alive, once she understands what is going on. Stanwyck received an Academy Award nomination as Best Actress in the role. The build-up of Burt's part, especially the flashbacks to his pre-married life, are gratuitous and disruptive, although he played the part well. The *Herald-Tribune*'s Barnes said Lancaster was 'grimly persuasive as the homicidal husband who gets caught in a mesh of telephone calls.' And *Look* magazine said: 'Burt Lancaster continues his steady advance from muscle-man to accomplished actor.'

And once again, Lancaster's name on the movie helped *Sorry, Wrong Number*'s box office by at least a million dollars, also a considerable amount in 1948.

Because of this economic leverage, and to be sure that he would always have his choice of roles, Burt and Harold Hecht went ahead with the formation of their production company, just two and a half years into his movie career, and the same amount of time ahead of their most optimistic prediction of five years. Lancaster incorporated himself as Norma Productions, named after his wife, and combined with Harold in Hecht-Norma as producers of their first co-venture, *Kiss the Blood Off My Hands*, also starring Burt as a Canadian merchant seaman, and Joan Fontaine as a nurse.

Lancaster was thus the first major movie star to begin his own independent production company since the 1920s, when Mary Pickford, Douglas Fairbanks, Charlie Chaplin and others even had their own studios to protect the profits from their pictures. Just prior to Lancaster's day 'Bing Crosby and Errol Flynn both had produced independent films, but those were inexpensive pictures, made at the height of their careers to turn a quick buck, mainly because of the tax concessions available at the time,' Burt noted. 'We were trying to develop a continuing company, and we were not primarily concerned with making money; our reason was the need for independence. I felt that Hollywood couldn't go on doing a lot of what was pure pap, as well as a lot of good films that were purely entertaining. People had to be given some of the realities of life. And, of course, in the years following the war, the USA was going through an enormous catharsis at all levels. Films in their own way are history-making. Like all good art they illuminate something.'

Hecht and Lancaster borrowed the money to make their first movie, and made a deal with Universal to distribute it. *Kiss the Blood Off My Hands* was taken from a novel by Gerald Butler, with a screenplay by Leonard

Bercovici, and directed by former actor Norman Foster. During the problem-plagued seven-week production schedule the title was thought to be a detriment and was changed often to *The Unafraid*, only to be changed quickly back to the original. Fontaine announced, shortly after production began, that she was in the early stages of pregnancy. She then caught cold and needed twelve days off to recover. The third lead, Robert Newton, had trouble adjusting to changes in the shooting schedule, which were brought on by unexpected rain as well as by Fontaine's illness. (The movie, although set in London, was shot in Hollywood, where rain is seldom a threat to exterior sequences and usually has to be manufactured when a screenplay calls for it.) Despite these problems, the fledgling producers Hecht and Lancaster completed *Kiss the Blood Off My Hands* in forty-eight days, just three more than the projected forty-five.

The movie tells the story of a merchant seaman (Lancaster), who is given to uncontrollable bursts of rage as a result of a beating in prison. He kills the owner of a London pub, then escapes into an apartment building, where he encounters Fontaine's nurse, who is somewhat tonier than her station in life would suggest; she agrees to help him stay hidden. Newton's character has witnessed the killing, however, and follows Lancaster to blackmail him into joining a highjacking scheme. Newton also makes advances to Fontaine, who kills him in self-defence and flees with Lancaster. The film's ads had the Fontaine character proclaiming, 'You're everything that's bad, but I've never loved any man like this.'

With the release of *Kiss the Blood Off My Hands*, which barely did better than break even, Burt Lancaster was beginning to have what would two decades later

[50]

become known as an 'image problem'. He had played at least one too many semi-sympathetic rotters to suit most critics. *The New York Times'* Thomas M. Pryor took the opportunity to turn his review of the picture into a treatise on its star-producer. Pryor wrote, in an article titled 'Lancaster Fights the World Again': 'The process of humanising Burt Lancaster is not going to be easy, and it is going to take time. [He] is handy with fists and speaks most eloquently when using them. But to develop fully as an actor and to come over to the right side of society he will have to make a break someday, for there are only so many variations on the theme of being misunderstood, and Mr Lancaster has just about exhausted them.'

Criss Cross, Lancaster's first movie of 1949, was hardly calculated to change the situation. 'As part of Mark Hellinger's estate settlement I was obliged to do this third picture for his company [inherited by Hellinger's widow, Gladys Glad]. It wasn't very good. It was done quickly and thrown into the melting pot.' Even Robert Siodmak as director didn't save it, because Hellinger had never completed a script. 'Mark had the original idea about the holding up of the race-track, and he had gone into an enormous amount of study as to how things should be done,' Burt remembered, 'things to do with the guards, and the handling of the trucks that come, and the switching back and forth of millions of dollars from the bank. He had an exciting *Rififi* approach to the whole thing. This half-finished version of *Criss Cross* reverted to Universal; they came up with a kind of rehashed chow of a script. Siodmak was in a position similar to me. He was obligated to do the film as part of his deal with the Hellinger estate. So we backed into a picture nobody really wanted to do, and the end result was a poor one.'

Yvonne De Carlo and Dan Duryea also starred in *Criss Cross*. Screenwriter Daniel Fuchs and Siodmak tried to remember and recreate Hellinger's concept, which the producer had outlined to them largely orally. What they came up with was a standard gangster tale, reminicent of *The Killers* in that a useless, heartless and thoughtless woman (De Carlo) manages to keep two men on her string for no reason stronger than her whim. A few powerful scenes invoke the earlier Hellinger-Lancaster-Siodmak collaboration, but even the crime itself is watered down from Hellinger's original conception: as filmed it is just a plain old pay-roll robbery. Once again, Lancaster is cast as the less-than–bright youth who agrees to join the job as a means of winning back his ex-wife, De Carlo, with whom he is still in love, but who is now married to the mob leader (Duryea). De Carlo does eventually turn away from Duryea and back to Lancaster, who by then has second thoughts about the heist and tries to turn his brutal cronies in. Duryea ends up killing both his wife and Lancaster.

This was understandably all too much – or too little, or too the same – for the *Herald-Tribune*'s James S. Barstow, Jnr who wrote: 'Lancaster is almost forced into a nearby parody of his previous dumb brute portrayals. He is given the thankless job of holding down a responsible job as an armoured car policeman and at the same time appearing stupid enough to be led by the nose by a floozie to an improbable group of criminals and his death.'

Director Siodmak was surprised and delighted by Burt during the making of *Criss Cross*. 'I thought I would find a different Lancaster,' he said. 'He's just the same except a better actor. He still fights me when he doesn't want to do a scene as I outline it. But he did before, too – when he knew nothing about pictures. You have to give him a reason for everything. Once you do, he's easy to handle. I thought that, because he had produced a picture himself just before *Criss Cross*, he might move in a little on my end. But he didn't; he stuck to acting and let me do the directing.'

Although the role of dumb, tough guy was beginning to bug Burt, Wallis continued to see it as good business. As soon as he got Lancaster back from the third and last Hellinger/Universal movie, Wallis cast him in *Rope of Sand*. This was a steamy melodrama set in the diamond mining district of South Africa. Wallis hired co-stars Claude Rains, Peter Lorre and Paul Henreid, hoping to recreate some of the feel and the box office success of their previous collaboration, *Casablanca*. Corinne Calvet, in her American movie debut, was cast in the Ingrid Bergman slot, and Lancaster was expected to do a Bogart as a big game hunter who competes with mine owners Rains and Henreid for a cache of diamonds. Calvet, as Rains's French mistress, is dispatched to distract Lancaster, of course, but ends up falling in love with him. The movie has an earthy sexiness that caused some problems with the Johnston Office, the Hollywood censors of the day. It has a distinctive Franz Waxman score, and some fine desert photography (Yuma, Arizona was the location), but *Rope of Sand* perhaps is better remembered as the last occasion on which Burt Lancaster did an acting job simply because Hal Wallis said he should.

Perhaps as an antidote to dumb crooks, Lancaster and Nick Cravat took their old acrobatic act out on the road for two weeks in 1949, with the Cole Brothers Circus, visiting several American cities, including their old stomping grounds of Chicago and New York. This time, however, they were paid $11,000 a week. A private railroad car with its own full-time chef was fitted out for them at a cost of $65,000 but, Burt recalled, 'After three days of that, I borrowed the manager's auto and drove from town to town. I couldn't stand all that comfort, and the food was too rich for my blood. Actually it wasn't so much fun going back.'

Lancaster was very conscious of, and at least a bit concerned about, his lingering image as a tough guy. But he wasn't so concerned as to court the press, especially columnists, which was a standard practice at the time. 'Look, Hopper,' he said to Hedda at the height of her power, when she asked him why he thought he should be a producer, 'let's get things straight right now. I don't frighten easily, and you don't scare me at all. I see right through you. I understand you perfectly, because you're just exactly like my mother.' Hopper took the comparison to his parent as a compliment, although he hadn't meant it as one.

'Don't bother me with any of these creepy newspaper people,' he would order his studio-assigned press agents. When columnist Sheilah Graham attempted to interview him on a movie set, he steered her towards the large community lunch table for cast and crew, then repeated each of her questions loudly to others. 'His replies were intended to – and did – embarass me. He was using me as a test pattern,' she said, 'to see how far he could go, to prove he was an independent man who could make fun of a columnist and to hell with the consequences.'

'To blazes with phony glamour,' Burt bellowed when he acquiesced to a rare magazine interview and a studio advisor suggested he shouldn't bounce his infant son Billy on his knee while the lady writer was attempting to fabricate a romantic fantasy about him for his female fans. In fact, Burt frequently broke with then prevalent film star convention by having his wife, father, and kids watch him on the set or join him for lunch in the studio commissary. He did notice that, as a result of his inaccessibility to fans, 'Most people seem to think I'm the kind of guy who shaves with a blow-torch. Actually, I'm inclined to be bookish and worrisome.'

Burt didn't go to Hollywood parties, and showed no carousing tendencies of any kind. He had a small group of friends with whom he played golf and bridge, and he still saw a great deal of Cravat and other circus friends. Former cronies from New York and Chicago or the army were always invited to his sets or his Bel-Air house, which few other movie stars ever got to see. 'I seldom take the children to a circus, and I don't go to nightclubs,' he said, 'I don't even go to premieres. Sometimes we go out for dinner, but my wife has to prod me to do that.'

'Marriage has steadied me down,' he added. 'My wife has good sound judgment and has the unbelievable wisdom of waiting until she is asked for an opinion. She has my unstinted admiration for her gift of restraint. After we married she said she'd had her professional fling [during the war] and was quite happy to sit on the sidelines while I had mine. She is very interested, too, in all my ambitions, so much so that I have named my company, Norma Productions, after her.'

For the next few years, Norma the company, in various combinations and with a name change or two, was to be an important force in independent production in Hollywood.

CHAPTER FIVE

Almost Forty and Almost Free

ROPE OF SAND signalled the end of Burt's Hollywood apprenticeship in several ways: his contract with Wallis was subject to renegotiation, and the renewal left Lancaster with as much creative freedom as any actor in American movies in 1950. Until then his film-making had been confined to Paramount and Universal projects, either under the aegis of Wallis or of Hellinger's company. While Burt would make three more movies for Wallis, two of which he would have to fight for, the producer's influence over him was minimal from 1950 on. Lancaster and Hecht now had all of Hollywood open to them. The partners signed a contract with Warner Brothers, which allowed them to use Burt strictly as a star in one of their movies for each film he and Harold made with Warner Brothers as co-producers – for a total of three of each kind.

Since his star stature also enabled Burt to make deals as a freelance actor, with only token approval from Wallis, he was mentioned for many major roles at other studios. And there were attempts to lure him back to

Broadway. 'It's ironic how one's career goes,' Lancaster recalled. 'I met Elia Kazan in New York and he and Tennessee Williams both wanted me to do *A Streetcar Named Desire* in the original Broadway production, but I had to go back to Hollywood for a film so Marlon Brando did it. I don't say that I would have done it as well as Brando, but I do think I would have been very good for that particular role, but I never got a chance to do it.'

Darryl Zanuck at Twentieth Century-Fox offered Lancaster the lead in *Twelve O'Clock High*. 'I wanted to do it,' Burt remembered, but I told him he'd have to make a three–picture deal with our company. He personally wasn't against the idea, but he said "New York'll never allow that. They won't give that authority." The deal fell through. Gregory Peck got the role.'

John Garfield was for a time, pre-production, a reluctant lead in the movie *The Breaking Point* and Lancaster was considered as a replacement. (Garfield finally came around and rejoined the project.) As a producer, Burt wanted to film Theodore Dreiser's *St Columba and the River*, and Norman Mailer's *The Naked and the Dead*. Even more, fresh on the heels of his return from the Cole Brothers Circus tour, Lancaster wanted to do *Advance Man*, the story of a circus press agent. He assured all concerned that this project would not in any way conflict with Cecil B. DeMille's circus epic then in the works: *The Greatest Show On Earth*. DeMille's movie got made and won an Oscar as Best Picture of 1952. Burt's never did get done.

Fortunately, the real beginning of Lancaster's career as a producer-actor was like nothing he had done before: *The Flame and the Arrow*. 'When we were making our production deal with Warner Brothers,' Burt recalled, 'we happened to mention to Jack Warner that we had this property, a script by Waldo Salt based on the William Tell story. It's worth noting that we originally brought the *Flame* script to Columbia, which wanted me to do a picture for them. We showed them Salt's screenplay and they said: "No, no, we want you to do a gangster picture." They thought I was in the general ilk since I'd made *Brute Force*, *I Walk Alone* and *Criss Cross*. I was anxious to get into something different. But Jack had his people read it and called us back in. "Why don't we do this one first," he said. "We've got all the *Robin Hood* sets here that we can use." And that's what we did.'

In *The Flame and the Arrow*, Burt finally got to demonstrate on screen some of the acrobatic agility that had been part of his publicity package since coming to Hollywood. No one, not even Flynn, from the time of Douglas Fairbanks, Snr, Lancaster's earliest idol, had leapt about, swung from chandeliers, climbed poles, scaled walls or fought with swords in the way Burt did in this departure picture. Lancaster put his pal Nick Cravat in the movie as his equally acrobatic but mute sidekick; the non-speaking part made it easier to cover Cravat's lack of acting experience – except of course as a 'dumb actor' in circuses. Lancaster starred as Dardo, 'The Arrow', a daredevil mountain man in eleventh century Lombardy, who – among other things – rescues a fair maiden (Virginia Mayo) from her Hessian family, who are invaders of the Italian province.

By 1950, Errol Flynn was too old to undertake strenuous physical roles. But Lancaster was happy to oblige, not only on the sets of Flynn's *The Adventures of Robin Hood*, but also utilising the set built for Flynn's more recent *The Adventures of Don Juan*. One important difference between the stars was that Lancaster did all his own stunt work, as Warner Brothers widely advertised. And while the style of the film was similar to those of Fairbanks and Flynn, and even reminiscent of silent movie slapstick, *The Flame and the Arrow* was in the vanguard of screen spoofs of action-oriented heroes. 'Previous to this, the early Fairbanks films and later the Errol Flynn films, played the swashbuckling thing dead straight,' Burt opined. 'There was a certain amount of humour in the films of course, but they were very serious about everything. I daresay we were the innovators of camping up that type of thing, which later became famous in the Bond series. We had scenes in the movie that Jack Warner threw up his hands over. As the first camp swashbuckler it had a lot of spoofing and *schtick*, funny bits of business. Warner shook his head and exclaimed, "What the fuck is this, *Midsummer Night's Dream?*"

'There was a publicity thing offering a reward to anybody who could prove I didn't do my own stunts in the film,' Burt recalled. 'I had to go to court over it because an extra made such a claim. Technically speaking, I didn't do all the shots. While I was busy elsewhere, somebody else might have been called in to work in some long shots. I was able to show that that did not constitute stunt work. Actually, the whole thing was a little suspicious, though I hadn't realised that before we went to court. Warner Brothers wasn't about to risk a million bucks, so they used a little legal trickery in stating their announcement. The judge told us that it was terribly naughty, but he was amused by it all.' (Don Turner, the extra in question, claimed he had been involved in three separate stunt sequences, but even he did not attempt to take credit for the strictly acrobatic scenes of high-bar walking and high-pole balancing that Burt did with Cravat, as they had so many times before.)

A Max Steiner score for *The Flame and the Arrow* further enhanced the illusion of an Errol Flynn film, but Lancaster brought an elan of his own to the colour feature directed by Jacques Tourneur. *Flame* was an instant hit on release, making a lot of money for Hecht-Norma and Warner Brothers, and giving Burt himself even more clout and influence in the industry. In an astute business decision, Lancaster uncharacteristically went out on tour to promote the picture, doing live gymnastics of the sort he had done for the camera – thereby further dispelling any doubt about his having done the stunts, while drumming up additional business at the box office. When asked, during the tour, why he had taken the risk both on and off camera, Burt replied, 'I've got a couple of thousand bucks in that picture – what's a neck?'

The reviews for *The Flame and the Arrow* were virtually unanimous raves, even that of the previously unimpressed Bosley Crowther in *The New York Times*. 'Not since Douglas Fairbanks was leaping from castle walls and vaulting over the rooftops of storybook towns has the screen had such a reckless and acrobatic young man to display these same inclinations as it has in Mr Lancaster.'

Once they had a hit, of course, 'Columbia called us back. This time we wanted to sell them a poignant story about a returning serviceman's attitude towards his new baby,' Lancaster remembered. 'Again the Columbia boys turned us down: "No, no you don't understand. We want you to do a movie like *The Flame and the Arrow*." The Hollywood mentality. You work against it all the time.'

Lancaster was looking for a new challenge, and

hoped for his next non-Hecht-Norma Warner Brothers picture to do the life story of William Lurye, the International Ladies Garment Workers Union official who was murdered violently by hoodlums. The studio decided that this subject matter would not lend itself to 'viable entertainment'. Hal Wallis wanted to reunite Lancaster with Lizabeth Scott in *Dark City*, but lucrative loan-out offers came from Twentieth Century-Fox and Metro-Goldwyn-Mayer for Burt's services, and Wallis did not want to turn them down. Thus, while Lancaster went off to do *Mr 880* for Fox and *Vengeance Valley* for MGM, Wallis assigned his new male contractee, Charlton Heston, to *Dark City*, Heston's major movie debut. (When Wallis was first interested in signing Heston from Broadway, an associate described the actor as 'another Burt Lancaster'. The producer paused only briefly before replying, 'Yes, but do we need another Burt Lancaster?')

Mr 880 was 'a small picture, a kind of sweet little film with Dorothy McGuire and Edmund Gwenn', in Lancaster's words. The sentimental storyline had Gwenn as the title character, an old man who made very bad counterfeit one-dollar bills (the unlikely small denomination was so as not to steal more than he actually needed), but who nonetheless had escaped capture for more than a decade. Lancaster is the US Treasury agent assigned to arrest the counterfeiter, while McGuire is a United Nations translator unknowingly involved with both the hunted and the hunter. It is Gwenn's movie, and he dominated it as surely as he had *Miracle on 34th Street* (for which he won an Oscar as Santa Claus) three years earlier. Gwenn was again nominated for a Supporting Actor Oscar in *Mr 880*.

Vengeance Valley, Lancaster's first western, was filmed by MGM on location in Colorado's Rocky

Mountains as well as at the Culver City studios. It is admirable in its attempts at authenticity regarding the actual workings of a ranch, especially in its scenes of cowboys conducting the spring cattle round-up. Lancaster plays the foster brother of Robert Walker, who gets a local waitress (Sally Forrest) pregnant and attempts to take over his father's (Ray Collins) ranch, blaming Burt for these and other wrongdoings. Walker ends up dead, after a fatal encounter with Lancaster, which was called for by the Production Code of 1951: the bad must always be punished before the final fade-out. Lancaster, still a New York street kid when it came to riding a horse, but athletic enough to adapt to the new sport, settled into the saddle over the course of the next decade and eventually looked as comfortable in one as any movie star cowboy.

Jim Thorpe, the Oklahoma Indian athlete who set pentathlon and decathlon records at the 1912 Olympics (only to be stripped of his medals when it came out that he had played professional baseball), had declined into drinking and drifting since the death of a son. He had arrived in Hollywood in the 1940s and was reduced to working as an extra and in bit parts in movies, usually as a stereotyped Indian. Thorpe had written an autobiography with Russell Birdwell, to which Warner Brothers acquired the film rights. The studio held the rights for years awaiting the right actor to play the title part. Lancaster, except for the colour of his hair (which he blackened), was not only ideal, he was under contract to Warner Brothers. Burt, as perhaps the only movie star with sufficient athletic and dramatic credentials to portray Thorpe, was especially intrigued by the racial prejudice aspects of the story. Thorpe himself was hired as a technical adviser on *Jim Thorpe – All American*.

'He was at the time in pretty dire financial straits,' Lancaster recalled. 'There was even a move by the producers to get his medals back; it would have been a perfect ending for the movie. My only personal contact with him during the filming was when he did drop-kicking. He came out of the stands and tried to teach me. It was sort of touching. His life had gone to pot. His wife had opened a bar during the filming and the producers went crazy and bought her out.' Thorpe died on 28 March 1953.

The film's script, by Douglas Morrow and Everett Freeman, reduced Thorpe's three marriages to one (Phyllis Thaxter played his wife), and his six children to one. While his track-and-field triumphs are emphasised, his prowess at boxing, swimming and golf are ignored. Still, *Jim Thorpe – All American* remains reasonably faithful to the broad outlines of Thorpe's biography: his leaving the Oklahoma reservation to attend an Indian school in Pennsylvania, where his sports ability was spotted by coach Pop Warner (Charles Bickford), his elusive championships and gradual spiritual deterioration. Michael Curtiz directed what remains one of the most commendable movies ever made about sport, and Lancaster exhibited yet another side of his athleticism – on the track – as well as his deeply felt but heretofore unexpressed compassion for downtrodden minorities.

'In *Jim Thorpe* we didn't beat people over the head with the Indian problem,' said Burt. 'Thorpe had his bad breaks, but they weren't due to the fact that he was an Indian. As he realised in later life, his downfall as an athlete was largely brought on by weaknesses in his own nature – a feeling that the world was against him, unreasonable stubbornness, and the failure to understand the necessity of working as a member of a team.'

In 1982, Thorpe's two Olympic gold medals were restored posthumously by the International Olympic Committee. Lancaster was not entirely mollified. 'I felt a certain cynicism that he didn't get them before,' Burt said. 'What does it mean now? There is a feeling of bitterness that it didn't get done in his own time.' (In 1983 Thorpe's grandson Bill Thorpe was named a torch carrier for the 1984 Summer Olympics in Los Angeles.)

Finally Hecht-Norma and Columbia were able to get together on a project: *Ten Tall Men*, a tongue-in-cheek story of a French Foreign Legion squad assigned to thwart an expected attack on their headquarters city. They kidnap a tribal chieftain's daughter (Jody Lawrence), which leads to countless fights and chases through sandstorms, accomplished with more than a hint of slapstick; in short, a Saharan swashbuckler. Lancaster decribed the movie as 'a spoof of the French Foreign Legion, a fairly successful picture as far as money was concerned. They never showed it in France, of course. The French might not have been too amused.' The success of *Ten Tall Men* convinced Lancaster and Hecht to produce another swashbuckler right away, this time back at Warner Brothers.

The Crimson Pirate was Lancaster's first film shot in Europe, to take advantage of lower production costs and some of the studio's frozen assets. Interiors were done in London, with most of the exteriors filmed in the Mediterranean and off the small island of Ischia in the Bay of Naples. It was the beginning of Burt's love affair with Italy. Although Robert Siodmak was brought back as director, this time there was no question that the producer-actor was the boss. At one point Lancaster startled Siodmak by shouting at him in front of the cast

[65]

and crew. 'You silly old has-been – this isn't the way the camera should be.' Lancaster even began quarrelling with Nick Cravat, who again had been cast (this time with second-billing) as the hero's mute sidekick.

A spoof of 'greater extremes' than *The Flame and the Arrow*, *The Crimson Pirate* is an all-out satire of the genre. 'I designed all the action sequences for *The Crimson Pirate*,' Lancaster remembered, 'all the comedy stuff. I worked with a comedy writer as well as with Siodmak himself. As a matter of fact, the whole last part of the film, the fight on the ship, which runs eighteen minutes of screen time, with all the gags and jokes, was shot by a writer [Roland Kibbee] and myself while Siodmak was in London shooting interiors for another part of the film.'

The storyline is almost superfluous: a sixteenth-century pirate is employed by Spaniards to put down revolutionaries on an island in the West Indies; the buccaneer jumps to the side of the rebels simply because their leader has a beautiful daughter (Eva Bartok). Lancaster termed *The Crimson Pirate* 'the first anti-establishment film – those pirates were really the good guys'. But despite its success with audiences, Burt knew better that anybody that it was time for an even more drastic change of direction as an actor than he had attempted at any time before. 'I'll go on making swashbucklers for my own company,' he said in 1952, after the release of *The Crimson Pirate*, 'but in my outside pictures I want to do things that will help me as an actor against the time when I have to give up all the jumping around.'

Wallis, to whom Lancaster was still under contract, bought the movie rights to William Inge's successful Broadway play, *Come Back, Little Sheba*. Shirley Booth, the actress acclaimed in the play's leading role of a wistful middle-aged slob who has emasculated her husband, was surprisingly hired to recreate the part on film – although she had never made a movie before and Wallis was thought to be taking a huge risk. The producer explained Booth's casting thus: 'She was a great actress; few others would have dared look so unattractive, and they would have compromised. Shirley never did. I decided to bring this hugely successful play to the screen. Up to now, Paramount executives had agreed with everything I wanted to do, but they were appalled by the idea of filming *Come Back, Little Sheba*. Prepared to accept glamorous men and women in melodramas of the seamy side of life, they were shocked at the thought of making a picture with beaten, unkempt, depressing people. Even the young people in the story were unattractive, morally if not physically: the tough girl who taunts the old woman, the muscular young stud who provides an unhappy sexual contrast with the defeated washout of a husband.'

Lancaster asked for the part of the husband, only to be told by Wallis, 'You're not right for it; you're too young.' 'I had to agree with Wallis, really,' Burt recalled, 'because the man in *Come Back, Little Sheba* should have been about sixty. But it was a part I wanted to play more than any other I ever got close to. Doc Delaney is the most human, if imperfect, kind of guy ever written into a play or script. I prevailed on Wallis. I said, "I understand this character. I'd like to play it. Now, we both know that it's Shirley's film – she's got the lead. But if I can do a respectable job in it, I will lend some weight to the box office for you."

That argument was persuasive, and Lancaster got the part, knowing he would have to do more than whiten his hair and add age lines to play it. He had formed his enthusiasm for the role only from reading the screenplay. 'I purposely didn't see the play,' he said, 'because I had my own ideas of how Doc should be portrayed. My agent said, "Why do you want to do this film? The role is secondary, you play the part of an older man who's a drunk, you're not right for it." I said, "I think you're right, but I understand this man and it's an opportunity to broaden myself as an actor." I didn't care about being, as they call it, a "second banana".'

As he had with *Sorry, Wrong Number*, Lancaster saw the husband not as a weakling, but as a strong man debilitated by his wife over a period of years. The story of *Come Back, Little Sheba*, as adapted by Ketti Frings from Inge's play, is the story of a marriage begun only because the woman, Lola, becomes pregnant. She miscarries and the couple remain childless. 'Doc' abandons his medical studies and becomes a chiropractor and increasingly alcoholic. Lola merely becomes older, more desperate in her yearning for both her lost youth and her lost dog, Sheba, whom she is convinced will return to her. The couple take in a pretty lodger (Terry Moore), who with her boyfriend (Richard Jaeckel), gives 'Doc' some yearnings of his own, and even more reason to drink. One night in an alcoholic rage he goes after Lola with a knife.

Wallis termed hiring Lancaster for this unlikely role, 'because of his great box office appeal', hedging only one bet. 'It was difficult for this huge, virile man to look like a weakling. We dressed Burt in a sloppy, shapeless button-up sweater, padded his figure to flab out his trim waistline, and gave him baggy trousers that made him look hip-heavy. He wore pale make-up over a stubble beard, but we still had a problem hiding his magnificent physique. We made him stoop a little, hollow his chest, and walk with a slow scuffle in

[68]

bedroom slippers. Burt went along with everything. Many male stars would have resisted, fearing that so unattractive an appearance might damage them in the eyes of their fans. But the good side of his cool confidence made any such loss of popularity unthinkable.'

During filming Shirley Booth said to Lancaster, 'Burt, once in a while you hit a note of truth and you can hear a bell ring, but most of the time I can see the wheels turning and your brain working.' But Lancaster said of her, 'Shirley Booth is the finest actress I have ever worked with . . . And I would put Magnani next – really superb artists, these two women. You're awed working with them, they're so good. *Come Back, Little Sheba* was a bold departure for me, to say the least. I don't fool myself for one moment, though. It was Shirley's picture and she was marvellous – and so it should have been hers. Because Bill Inge had written about this kind of woman, and how she was smothering and destroying this man without ever realising it, because she was the soul of kindness, so she thought. But I got extraordinarily interesting reviews for the first time. The tendency of the reviewer is to regard you in the image you have had before. In other words, I was the leading man or the swashbuckler, blah, blah, blah, and suddenly they were beginning to think of me as a serious actor. So that was a progression in my career.'

While *The New York Times*'s Bosley Crowther wrote, 'the excellence of Mr Lancaster as the frustrated, inarticulate spouse, weak-willed and sweetly passive, should not be overlooked', Lindsay Anderson said, in *Sight and Sound*, 'Lancaster is an actor of instinctive sensitivity, whose playing has always had a certain gentleness and sensibility. But his range is limited, and this difficult part goes beyond it. In the simple matter of age he is quite wrong, and the heavy lines of make-up and the whitened hair do not convince.'

Shirley Booth won the Best Actress Oscar for 1952, in her movie debut. For his part, Burt felt he had discovered the qualities that would put him among the top rank film talent, a select group he was about to join. 'An actor has got to have certain things going for him,' he said, 'if he's a truly great actor. I could describe the quality as something innate in him, something that in a sense has nothing to do with any qualifications or experience he might have: it's just God-given talent. On the other hand, a very good actor has to be intelligent, has to be sensitive and has to have some kind of strength. That applies to women too. A good actress has 'balls' in addition to heart and mind. For myself, I had a pretty varied background. I was an avid reader; I lived at opera and concerts. I wasn't the little boy coming to town from some place like South Dakota, who looked as if he'd just walked off the farm. I was born in New York and I'd spent all my life there, and it's a very sophisticated city. I had a reasonable knowledge of the political aspect of things too. So, with these qualities I was able to look at a script and see the values in it.'

Yet for all his success, particularly in athletic roles, Lancaster was beginning to have his doubts about going on with the acting part of his profession: 'As I approach forty, I'm beginning to ask, is being a movie star at that age worth the trouble? I don't think it is. It seems I've spent all my life in gyms. I've grown to hate training. I can't go on being the caricature of a he-man. I want simply to be a man and enjoy life as others do. Battling a losing game doesn't go with intelligent living. That's why I'm working my way into production. I asked myself what happens to people when they have nothing to do. They become a lonely burden to themselves and others.'

On the other hand, working with Booth in *Come Back, Little Sheba* had made Lancaster aware of the potential satisfaction in acting out a worthwhile script. For the next thirty years he would threaten to give up acting, to spend full time producing (or even directing), only to be attracted by what he considered a good piece of writing, and recanting. 'Too many actors forget that the play's the thing,' he said. 'I'm not interested in stealing a picture. I simply want to be in a good one. I've earned the reputation with directors of being a difficult man to work with. I don't want to run the show, but if I feel that a scene is going wrong, I want to do everything in my power to correct it, even if it means an argument with the director. Not my ego, but the picture is involved. In *Ten Tall Men* I worked with a girl relatively new to the screen. I'm sure many people couldn't understand why I spent so much time helping her do the best job possible. I wasn't particularly concerned with her as a person or with her career. I simply knew that if she looked bad, the scenes would fall flat, and I'd look bad too.'

Singing in *The Kentuckian*, 1955

With Anna Magnani, *The Rose Tattoo*, 1955

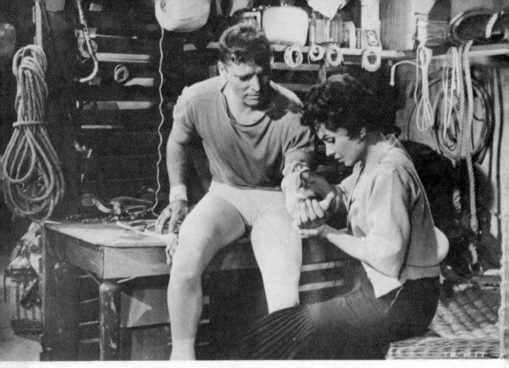

With Gina Lollobrigida, *Trapeze*, 1956

Gunfight at the OK Corral, 1957

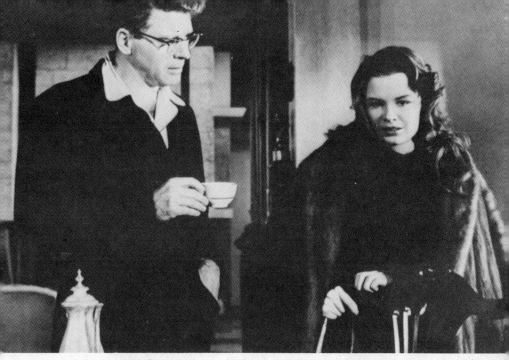

With Susan Harrison, *Sweet Smell of Success*, 1957

With Rita Hayworth, *Separate Tables*, 1958

With Dean Jagger and Jean Simmons in *Elmer Gantry*, 1960

Birdman of Alcatraz, 1962

The Leopard, 1963

With director Luchino Visconti

The Leopard, with Claudia Cardinale

With Jeanne Moreau, *The Train*, 1965

With John Anderson, *The Hallelujah Trail*, 1965

With Lee Marvin, *The Professionals*, 1966

With son Bill, on the set of TV's
The Big Valley, 1967

CHAPTER SIX

From Here to Eternity

HECHT AND LANCASTER, in 1952, produced their first of five movies not starring Burt: what was then known as a 'programme comedy', appropriately titled *The First Time*. It starred Barbara Hale and Robert Cummings as parents of a first baby, and was narrated by the infant, who described the problems of having them as parents. Frank Tashlin, who wrote the screenplay with three collaborators, also directed. Harold Hecht was listed as sole producer, and Lancaster had little to do with the innocuous black-and-white picture, which made slight impressions either critically or commercially. In order to get Lancaster for *Ten Tall Men*, Columbia President Harry Cohn had agreed to have his studio release *The First Time*.

Lancaster still had a few contractual obligations of his own: he agreed to make his television debut on a programme hosted by Hal Wallis's newest discoveries, Dean Martin and Jerry Lewis, NBC-TV's *Colgate Comedy Hour*. Burt appeared in a comedy sketch with Martin and Lewis. Warner Brothers was owed two more movies; the studio insisted that Lancaster star, again with Virginia Mayo, in the low-budget, black-and-white and witless *South Sea Woman.* 'I had to do it,' Burt explained. 'I owed Warners and this is what they picked. By this time Warners and I had soured on each other; I wanted to get out of my contract quickly and they were willing to let me go. I couldn't change their minds, so we rushed in and did *South Sea Woman* very quickly. It was a terrible picture.'

In *South Sea Woman* Lancaster plays a Marine sergeant in Honolulu, pre-Pearl Harbour, who tries to save his buddy from his love for the island-hopping strumpet of the title (Mayo), only to fall for her himself. Chuck Connors, an ex-football player who had just made his movie debut in John Wayne's *Trouble Along the Way* and would later gain fame as television's *The Rifleman*, was cast as the second leatherneck. The story is a strange combination of Marine derring-do and knockabout farce (at one point Lancaster cavorts in a grass skirt). The two volatile servicemen sieze a German yacht (killing the crew and freeing the French passengers), sink a Japanese destroyer, cause a Chinese junk to go up in flames, and repel an attack on Guadalcanal. Bosley Crowther in *The New York Times* summed up the movie as 'a terrible lot of nonsense'.

During the shooting of *South Sea Woman*, Warner Brothers enlisted Lancaster to do an unbilled cameo appearance in the studio's *Three Sailors and a Girl*, a Gordon MacRae-Jane Powell musical. For the bit, which took only two hours, Burt was even able to stay in his Marine uniform. In the finale of *Three Sailors and a Girl*, Lancaster appears backstage and says to Sam Levene, his erstwhile Broadway co-star from *A Sound of Hunting:* 'You'll never make it in show business, kid.' Burt's turn didn't help the picture, but it did help him in further

[74]

fulfilling his obligation to Warner Brothers – he had appeared in yet another of their movies.

His last film released by Warner Brothers, *His Majesty O'Keefe*, was also the last picture produced by Hecht-Norma, and Burt's last swashbuckler ever. Unlike *South Sea Woman*, which was made on the studio's back lot, Lancaster and company spent four months filming on location on the Fiji island of Viti Levu. Burt played an enterprising Yankee freebooter in the South Seas in the 1870s, who is thrown overboard by a mutinous crew. He swims to the island, where he concludes that a fortune can be made in local copra, if he can overcome the island's German traders, slave dealers and native superstition and apparent unwillingness to work. By the time he beats all those odds, his own priorities have changed; he falls in love with a half-caste Polynesian (played by British starlet Joan Rice), and accepts the islanders' offer to become their king. The hokey screenplay, based loosely on a real-life story, by Borden Chase and Hecht-Norma's new story editor, James Hill, was well-captured along with the lush setting, in Technicolor by *The Crimson Pirate*'s Otto Heller. Critics cited Lancaster's 'unflaggingly energetic playing' in *His Majesty O'Keefe*.

In the midst of all these loose ends, Lancaster delivered the finest and most important performance of his career to date, 1953, that of Sergeant (again!) Milton Warden in *From Here to Eternity*. To get Burt for the part, Harry Cohn at Columbia had to engage in complicated horse trading with Hal Wallis, involving other actors and scripts. Depending upon the values placed on the various properties, Cohn 'paid' Wallis between $200,000 and $300,000 for Lancaster's services, of which Burt received only about $100,000, and that only after a lot of complaining. (Lancaster had long been demanding bonuses beyond his basic salary, but Wallis granted them grudgingly and sparingly.) Wallis profited from the difference, including a $40,000 producer's fee he extracted from Columbia to film *Bad for Each Other* with his contractees Charlton Heston and Lizabeth Scott.

'*From Here to Eternity* was an enormous turning point for me,' Lancaster recalled. 'It was a great success, both critically and with audiences. I remember so well the first scene I did with Montgomery Clift. It was the first time – the only time this ever happened to me in my entire experience – that I couldn't stop my knees from shaking. He had so much power, so much concentration. Thank God the camera was only shooting above my waist. But after that it was fine and we became very good friends. Clift was a complicated man, there's no question about that. He and Frank Sinatra would get roaring drunk every night after filming. I spent so much time carrying them to their bedrooms, and undressing them, putting them into bed night after night. To this day Sinatra calls me "mom". He'll find me on my birthday, no matter where I am and say "Happy Birthday, Mom".'

Lancaster's Sergeant Warden, a tough career soldier based in Honolulu in the summer of 1941, was *From Here to Eternity*'s leading character. Burt's performance also revealed a compassionate side to the organised and dedicated NCO who refuses to pursue a commission because he has contempt for officers as a breed. But there were several other memorable portrayals in the Daniel Taradash adaptation of James Jones's mammoth (nearly half a million words) bestseller: Clift as the non-violent individualist, Private Prewitt; Sinatra as the feisty Maggio; Donna Reed as a high-class prostitute; Ernest Borgnine as a sadistic stockade sergeant; and above all, Deborah Kerr, as the commander's wife with whom Lancaster has an affair that is at first physical, then tender and loving, but always ill-fated. The scene in which Lancaster and Kerr make love on the beach in their bathing suits, as the surf breaks over them, remains one of the most vivid scenes in the movies, even thirty years later; in 1953 it was a breakthrough for the depiction of passion and sensuality in films. 'That was so erotic', Lancaster recalled, 'yet we didn't need to strip off to get the message over. I saw the TV series they made of it. It wasn't bad, but they couldn't match that movie.'

Jones's novel had been a bitter attack on American military life before World War II, with its cruelties, constraints and corruption, and their effect on servicemen. Taradash and director Fred Zinnemann were able to convey some of the tone and scope of Jones's condemnation within the two-hour movie melodrama. That achievement, along with the performances, earned *From Here to Eternity* a total of eight Academy Awards for 1953, including Best Picture, Best Screenplay for Taradash and Best Director for Zinnemann. Sinatra and Reed captured the supporting acting Oscars, and *From Here to Eternity* was also honoured for its sound recording, black-and-white cinematography, and editing. Kerr lost out as Best Actress, although she was nominated, to Audrey Hepburn in *Roman Holiday*. Both Clift and Lancaster were nominated as Best Actor, among the picture's total of thirteen nominations. But the Oscar for Best Actor that year went to William Holden for yet another military portrayal, in *Stalag 17*. The New York Film Critics, with their usual independence of Hollywood, named Lancaster Best Actor for the first of four times.

From Here to Eternity was also a major commercial

success, solidifying Lancaster's status as a top box office star. He also earned the respect of serious moviemakers and moviegoers with the reviews he received for his acting as Sergeant Warden. Typical was the rave by A.H. Weiler in *The New York Times:* 'In Burt Lancaster the producer [also Zinnemann] has got a top kick to the manner born, a man whose capabilities are obvious and whose code is hard and strange but never questionable. His view of officers leaves him only with hatred of the caste, although he could easily achieve rank, which would solve his romantic problem. But he is honest enough to eschew it and lose the only love he has known.'

Lancaster himself was especially proud of his work in *From Here to Eternity*. He cited his ability to control his anger, at least on screen, in the scene 'where Ernest Borgnine pulls out a knife and I break a bottle and stand there, facing him. It would have been easy just to snarl, "All right, you son-of-a-bitch". But I didn't do it that way. I just said quietly, "come on, come on". And it was twice as effective. When the scene was over, Monty Clift came over and put his arms around me. He was a sweet man, Monty, very emotional. He thought it was a great scene. I have to say I was very effective and forceful in that film.'

Burt clearly no longer needed co-production deals with Warner Brothers – which was suddenly, as a result of *From Here to Eternity*, eager to retain him – or anyone else. He and Hecht changed the name of their company from Hecht-Norma to Hecht-Lancaster in 1954, and set up offices at the Samuel Goldwyn Studios since they had signed a distribution agreement with the newly revitalised United Artists, which had its offices at Goldwyn. (Mary Pickford and Charles Chaplin had sold the company they co-founded with D.W. Griffith and

Douglas Fairbanks, Snr in 1919, to a group of New York movie men headed by Arthur Krim.) *Apache* was Hecht-Lancaster/United Artists' first effort, with Robert Aldrich directing Lancaster and Jean Peters as Indians in a story based on a book by Paul I. Wellman. Wellman's novel, in turn, was based on historical fact: Massai (Lancaster) was an Apache warrior who refused to surrender along with Geronimo in the 1880s, and continued to fight a one-man war against the white United States federal government. *Apache* was a first for Hollywood at that point: an attempt to depict the American Indian as more than a savage villain, as a deserving underdog. Neither are the whites in *Apache* unambiguous bad guys. James R. Webb, *Apache's* screenwriter, would deal with the same theme more ambitiously a decade later, in *Cheyenne Autumn*.

'Massai was a fierce, fighting Apache who hated the white man,' Lancaster remembered. 'We fictionalised the story a bit; he was so unrelenting and driving that he was almost too one-dimensional. We manufactured a story built on the legend. In the original ending of *Apache* I was killed by Charlie Bronson. We shot an alternative ending because the distributors said, "Burt, you can't die in a film." That's kind of what the Hollywood scene is about sometimes. And it wasn't just them: the exhibitors came with bended knees, saying, "Please don't die, your fans don't want to see you die." I must say that although I hated the idea, I went along with them and the picture was very successful, so I will never know how the other ending would have done.'

Apache, a wide-screen Technicolor movie, was produced for a budget of $900,000, and grossed over $6,000,000, considerably helping the new United Artists' cash flow. But the picture was less successful with the critics, who particularly objected to a blue-eyed blond Indian (albeit in a black wig). *Time* said that the colourful Western gave 'one-time Circus Acrobat Lancaster plenty of opportunities to leap daringly from crag to crag, horse to horse, and frying pan to fire', and *Variety* proclaimed both Peters and Lancaster 'outstanding'. But Howard Thompson in *The New York Times* said that Lancaster's production company had come up with its first 'clinker', and Britain's *Film Monthly Bulletin*, while noting *Apache*'s good intentions, said '. . . We remain conscious that these are two actors doing a very decent best in an impossible task. The strangeness is missing: Indians are not just white Americans with a different-coloured skin and a simplified vocabulary.'

Although director Robert Aldrich had found Lancaster 'not an easy man to get along with, but quite responsive', they quickly re-teamed on *Vera Cruz*, Hecht-Lancaster's next movie, timed for release at Christmas of 1954. This story of two American adventurers (played by Lancaster and Gary Cooper) who escort a French countess (Denise Darcel) from the Emperor Maximilian's Mexico City court to the port of Vera Cruz in 1866, was filmed entirely on location by Ernest Laszlo, in SuperScope and Technicolor, with a budget of $1,700,000. Although Burt had specialised to some extent in male-'bonding' movies, *Vera Cruz* was the first in which he co-starred with – and took second billing to – a top male star. Cooper, who was estimated to have added $2,000,000 to the picture's total $11,000,000 take, was not even Lancaster's first choice.

'I thought that the villain's role would have been sensational for Cary Grant,' Burt recalled, 'so I went to see him while he was visiting Grace Kelly on a Hitchcock set. He was very nice about it, but he turned me down. "I don't go near horses," he said. "I can't stand horses." I said, "It'd be such a departure for you, Cary. It's a good script written in a mocking vein. It's a *Gunga-Din* type of thing." I told him I would be his straight man. But he wouldn't do it. So we sent the script to Gary Cooper, and he liked it very much and agreed to do the straight role. But mine was the entertaining part. It was fun, playing that kind of character.'

Lancaster, playing the first out-and-out villain of his career, and thereby taking a big chance in commercial terms, and Cooper in a somewhat more heroic role, discover that Darcel is carrying a cache of gold to finance additional troops for Maximilian. The trio get very involved in double-crossing each other, and the two men change sides, according to which is paying the most at the moment. Finally, Cooper decides that the gold belongs to the Mexican people, and guns down his grinning partner, Lancaster, who wants to keep it for himself.

With their first two independent pictures for United Artists, *Apache* and *Vera Cruz*, smash hits on release, Hecht and Lancaster again began to look for properties that would not necessarily involve Burt as an actor. They acquired the motion picture rights to *Operation Heartbreak*, by Sir Alfred Duff Cooper, Viscount Norwich, the late First Lord of the Admiralty (in 1937-38). Alec Guinness was projected as the star, but the project never got out of the development stage.

But then, along came *Marty*, the Paddy Chayefsky story of a thirty-five-year-old Bronx butcher whose non-existent social life takes a decided turn for the better when he meets another plain-faced loner at a dance. *Marty* had already appeared on television, with Rod Steiger and Nancy Marchand in the leading roles, in a one-hour 'live' version that was preserved on a kine-scope. 'But even though the guys at United Artists were nice enough to admit that we just about made them,' Lancaster remembered, 'we had the devil of a time trying to get the money together to do *Marty* – even though it was an extremely small budget picture. They were dead set against *Marty*. "Who wants to see a picture about two ugly people?" they asked.

'My answer was that they should underwrite young talent like Paddy Chayefsky. They'd made enough from *Apache* and the Cooper movie was like money in the bank. Why shouldn't they be willing to lose a little, if at the same time they would be encouraging new writers, new ideas, new faces. They didn't do the movie for those reasons, though. They did it because I told them that if they didn't I wanted out of my contract. When it was all over they came to me and said, "Burt, we're glad we did the picture because we've won every award there is, and people are coming to UA with exciting ideas and *Marty* is worth its weight in gold, but . . ." And they got out the ledgers. There were theatres in small-town America that did only ten dollars worth of business in a day. With all the publicity and awards, *Marty* only grossed half of what *Vera Cruz* brought in. This was their argument. If a picture makes money it's successful. If it doesn't, forget about it. The fact is that it was a heartbreaking story and a beautiful film, but this is what you constantly run up against.'

Nonetheless, *Marty*, which cost a mere $330,000 to produce (the original budget was even less: $250,000), in black and white, was the long-shot hit of 1955. It made a star of character actor Ernest Borgnine as the butcher, and won him the Best Actor Oscar for that year. Betsy Blair, as his schoolteacher girlfriend, was nominated as Best Supporting Actress but lost to Jo Van Fleet in *East of Eden*. *Marty* won three Academy Awards in addition to Borgnine's: Best Picture, Best

Director for Delbert Mann, and Best Screenplay for Chayefsky. *Marty* grossed $5.5 million, exactly half the *Vera Cruz* figure. 'From their point of view, United Artists had lost,' said Burt. Actually, he had expected to lose money on *Marty*. 'I have always had this splendid confidence in my own judgment,' Lancaster added. 'Funnily enough, I made *Marty* because I loved the script – not to make a fortune. In fact, I intended it to be a tax-loss operation. So I was groaning all the way to the bank.'

Marty allowed Hecht-Lancaster to arrive artistically as well as commercially. 'They were fun days and we set the town on its ear with every movie we did,' said Burt. 'We actually broke the rules.' While Lancaster sometimes made fun of his partner, a small man, calling him 'Lord Mole' (and Hecht's then-wife 'Lady Bird Legs' because of her skinny gams), in 1955 he was still thrilled to be his partner. 'Hecht and I complement each other,' Lancaster said. 'Harold is the best executive I ever saw and an exceptional critic. He's not creative, but infallible when it comes to knowing what's good. Jim Hill, our story man [not yet a full partner in the production company] is wonderful, and let me tell you, good material is the life and breath of this business. No actor can make a bad story good. We believe in getting top stories and are not afraid to pay for top talent.'

To prove it, Hecht-Lancaster hired A.B. Guthrie, Jnr at a high fee, to do the screen adaptation of Felix Holt's novel *The Gabriel Horn* as *The Kentuckian*. In addition to playing the leading role of a widower with a young son who finds 1820s Kentucky too confining and wants to trek west to Texas, Lancaster decided to make his directing debut in *The Kentuckian*. He already had the reputation of being difficult with his directors ('There's only one man worse than me for telling directors what to do,' said Kirk Douglas, 'and that's Burt'), and had said from the beginning of his Hollywood career that he wanted to direct. Here was his chance.

Despite Laszlo's excellent location photography, once again, and a stirring score by Bernard Herrmann, good performances in both large and small parts, *The Kentuckian* was sluggish and meandering. It takes an awfully long time for Lancaster's Big Eli to fall in love with a local schoolteacher (Diana Lynn), then with an indentured servant girl he has freed (Dianne Foster), who goes to work for a local sadist (Walter Matthau in his movie debut) in order to earn the money to pay Eli back. Only then, after murdering some local villains, can Eli, his son and his new wife begin to think about leaving for Texas. There is only one major action sequence in this ponderous Western, in which Lancaster with his bare fists fights Matthau wielding a bullwhip.

Variety called Lancaster's performance 'a bit too self-conscious, as though the director and the actor couldn't quite agree', while *The New York Times* said the movie had 'no sense of dramatic focus or control'. *Variety* added that 'more concentration on the meat of the plot, and less on unnecessary incidental detail could have kept the pace lively.' Yet, as Burt was quick to point out, he also got some very good reviews: '*Time* and *Life* wrote very nice things about my work as a director.'

Lancaster blamed the generally unenthusiastic reception for *The Kentuckian* (it also failed to generate much activity at the box office) on the screenplay as much as on anything else. 'It was a lovely idea, the story,' he said. 'We were never quite happy with the script, but we worked on it constantly during the actual shooting of the film, and when we got through we had what I think you could call a very pleasant little film. And that's about all that could be said for it.'

Being an actor-director, he found 'the hardest job of my life. I was taking on a lot; I knew that when I started. In addition to playing the leading role, in which I was in just about every scene, I had the problem of getting up terribly early in the morning, at five o'clock, to go out to the locations to set everything up. I never got to bed before midnight or one o'clock in the morning. I had to work with all the rushes and the editor, then sit up going over the scenes for the next day. I had no time for anything else. I never worked so hard in my life. It's no life really, being a director. Nobody works harder than a director, if he's at all serious. His work is never finished, simply never finished. You are married to your work. You're not only the first one on the set, but you work all day long, you make all the decisions, you deal with temperamental actors and actresses. Then the next day you start the same grind all over again. But it's the best job in pictures, because when you're a director, you are God. And you know that's the best job in town.'

Lancaster claimed that he was not particularly influenced in his own work on *The Kentuckian* by any of the directors with whom he had worked previously. 'I had always felt, though, that I had a kind of director's attitude toward my work. I was constantly worrying about the writing of the scripts I acted in, always wanting to change the staging of scenes, always feeling it could be done in a different way. I never lost that tendency. For some reason many directors find it difficult to work with me. But it's the way any actor works who's worth his salt. Very few actors just stand there and allow themselves to be directed. They're the ones who have to *do* it, so they have to have some concept as to what they want to do – some approach to it that will make their work that much more effective, and bring off the idea they're trying to express.'

Still, Lancaster said, 'It was very difficult for me, directing this picture. I had no one to help me, just struggled through on my own. Actually, I had a very good cameraman, but he was kind of a quiet guy, very artistic with his camera, but not the kind of person who really locks horns with you. And I like that, whether it's a director or another actor I'm dealing with. I learned it's no job to be a director; the tough job is being a good director. I will probably never again act in a picture I also direct. Much as I've enjoyed working as an actor in the past, it's possible I may quit that phase of show business and concentrate on being a director. That's been my real ambition. But the problem that I had in Hollywood, being known as an actor, was that no one would give me a job as a director. Fortunately, having my own company, I was able to direct a picture on my own.'

Lancaster never did quit acting, and he would not direct again for nineteen years; he was co-director and co-scenarist with Roland Kibbee on 1974's *The Midnight Man*, in which he also starred. In fact, his first work after *The Kentuckian* was strictly as an actor, for Hal Wallis, in a secondary role to a strong woman star again. 'I had to prevail on Wallis to let me do *The Rose Tattoo*, in which I got right away from the heroic character,' Lancaster recalled. 'I was a bubbling, cuddly sweet sort of person and Anna Magnani pushed him around until she finally came to realise that her life was better with him than it would be if she continued to keep up the illusion about her dead husband.'

Tennessee Williams had written the play *The Rose Tattoo* for Magnani in the first place, but the Italian actress had too little facility in English to attempt it on stage, abdicating the Broadway run to Maureen Stapleton. Williams then sold *The Rose Tattoo* to Hollywood with two stipulations: that he himself would write the screenplay (although Hal Kantor was brought in to assist with the adaptation); and that Magnani – whose English had improved dramatically – would star as Serafina, the fiery Italian–American widow who promises to remain faithful to the memory of her dead husband. *The Rose Tattoo* as a movie, like the play, would remain her vehicle. The dim, oafish but happy truck driver, Alvado Mangiacavallo, stirs her up and tempts her to break her vow, but not until nearly halfway through the movie – although Williams's plot depended on Alvado's virile resemblance to the deceased husband. 'Even though there was a great deal of prestige attached to the play, it wasn't usual Hollywood fare, and wasn't expensive to acquire,' Burt remembered. 'Wallis bought it, I was still under contract to him and asked to be in it.' Because Lancaster wanted the part so badly, Wallis 'was delighted to go along, since my participation added to the saleability of the film, just as it had with *Sheba*.'

The Rose Tattoo was filmed first at Paramount, then on location in Key West, Florida, next door to Williams's own home. Magnani refused to fly anywhere, so Williams sailed with her from Naples to New York, a trip that took two weeks, then travelled with her by train, first to Hollywood, then to Florida. He coached her in English all the way. On a train trip of his own that year, 1955, to Kansas City, with James Hill and Bob Schiffer, Burt's longtime make-up man (later head make-up man for Walt Disney Productions), Lancaster acquired one remarkable feature of his characterisation in *The Rose Tattoo*.

As Schiffer told the story, 'Burt and Hill were sitting opposite me in the restaurant car. Behind me sat a man and his wife. The woman had on a low-cut dress. Hill was eating olives, and he began to flick the stones over my shoulder. One finally went down the woman's dress. Burt didn't see any of this; he was spooning up his soup. The first he knows of it is that this man is standing over him, wanting to punch him, so Burt just stands up and is – magnificent. The next minute all hell is let loose. Burt's fighting the man. The conductor starts fighting me. Then they want to throw us off the train. We're in the middle of the bloody desert. All the time Hill is sitting there, sweet as pie, eating his olives. Anyway we finally talk our way out of it. So I'm fed up with these two idiots. Burt was on about his next film, *The Rose Tattoo*. I hadn't read the part or anything, but I said to him, "You can't play it with all that hair. He'd just done the Western and had all this long golden hair. I ended up cutting it all off to about a quarter of an inch – with nail scissors.'

Lancaster's role in the *The Rose Tattoo* (played on Broadway by Eli Wallach) called for him to play the clown to amuse Serafina, to the point of climbing a telephone pole. His Italian accent, though honestly come by from his old East Harlem neighbourhood, came out as slightly comic, making his performance seem highly contrived. He was physically right for the role. Eventually, especially after she learns her late husband had been unfaithful, Serafina accepts Mangia-cavallo as the new man in her life. In real life, at least according to Wallis, Magnani 'fell head over heels for her co-star. He was just her type of big, broad-should-ered he-man, but he wasn't attracted to her and she got nowhere and gallantly settled for friendship. Though they both had enormous egos, they were unselfish in their playing, and respected each other's talent.'

As expected, *The Rose Tattoo* was a tour-de-force for Anna Magnani, who easily won the Best Actress Oscar for 1955, the same year Borgnine won Best Actor and Harold Hecht Best Picture/Producer for *Marty*. James Wong Howe was also honoured by the Academy for his cinematography on *The Rose Tattoo*, and a third Oscar was given to the movie for art direction. Marisa Pavan was nominated as Best Supporting Actress for her vivid portrayal of Serafina's daughter, against Blair in *Marty* and winner Jo Van Fleet (East of Eden), who also appeared in *The Rose Tattoo*. The film did respectably at the box office. But Burt got reviews like Arthur Knight's in *The Saturday Review:* 'He attacks the part with zest and intelligence . . . But one is always aware that he is acting, that he is playing a part that fits him physically but is beyond his emotional depth. His strong-toothed grin, his cropped, slicked-back hair, his bent-kneed walk are, like his precarious Italian accent, mannerisms and devices carefully acquired for the occasion and barely more than skin deep. The earnestness of his effort only serves to highlight Magnani's own complete submergence in her role.'

CHAPTER SEVEN

Sweet Smell of Success

LANCASTER AND Shelley Winters had an affair during this most successful period of his career. He was married at the time, she was divorced from Vittorio Gassman, not yet married to Anthony Franciosa. On their first date, Burt and Shelley went to Le Pavillon, then one of New York's best and most expensive restaurants, for dinner, and to the Broadway musical *South Pacific*. Shelley's recollection of the events following, in his hotel room, was a little vague, but she recalled them lying on a thick white rug, 'and Burt didn't have any clothes on and he was gorgeous and I didn't have any clothes on and I felt gorgeous, and now Gigli was singing 'O Paradiso' on the phonograph . . . Cut to: A galloping army with banners, meteors flashing and a spangled sky . . . and the Top of the World.'

Winters wrote in her autobiography that this affair with Lancaster was one of her most chaotic but also one of her strongest, marred by the guilt she felt because he was married and had children. When it appeared in print that Lancaster's wife was expecting a fifth child, Winters decided to end the romance. She told Marlon Brando, 'I know in my heart it's true: that bastard's fucking his wife.' When Winters wound up in the hospital with a minor nervous breakdown, Lancaster sent her flowers and a cheque for $3,000. 'I told him to keep the roses,' she recalled, 'but I kept the $3,000 – my severance pay, I guess.'

Trapeze, filmed in Paris at the Cirque d'Hiver in 1956, proved to be Hecht-Lancaster's biggest success to date, grossing seventeen million dollars. It provided Burt with both a circus background at last, and a strong character part: he played an aerial acrobat who is injured in a fall before the opening credits of *Trapeze*, and is seen throughout the rest of the movie walking with a limp. Tony Curtis plays the up-and-coming acrobat who convinces Lancaster to coach him into the nearly impossible triple somersault, and Gina Lollobrigida is the opportunistic aerialist who, in turn, loved them both, or pretended she did. Lancaster brushed up on his acrobatics for *Trapeze* and Curtis and Lollobrigida learned some aerial stunts in order to minimise the need for doubling. Lancaster managed to do most of his own stunts but Eddie Ward of the Ringling Brothers Circus was hired to double Burt's most dangerous tricks and serve as technical adviser on *Trapeze*. Ward and Lancaster had worked together in the Gorman Brothers Circus in 1935.

'To give you an idea of how important we considered the script,' Lancaster said, 'we spent $100,000 for the writing on *Trapeze*.' Among the people who worked on the script, based on Max Catto's *The Killing Frost*, are Sam Taylor, who wrote *Sabrina*, James Jones (*From Here to Eternity*), Ernie Lehman (*Executive Suite*) and Ruth and Augustus Goetz. Pretty good names, and a lot of money to spend before you ever get into production.'

Carol Reed, the English director on *Trapeze*, was, according to Lancaster, 'marvellous, a very nice man, but my impression of him, right or wrong, is that he was not very articulate when it comes to talking about the story. He couldn't really pin down exactly what he wanted. He was brilliant in the use of the camera and could tell the story in a highly original way – look at *Odd Man Out* or *The Third Man* or *The Fallen Idol*, so beautiful to watch. But he didn't seem to come up with the right ideas for his stories.'

It is true that *Trapeze* is better remembered for its outstanding action sequences rather than for its screenplay. Lancaster, who can no longer perform the tricks that made him famous is persuaded by Curtis to become his trainer, and 'catcher', which the injured older performer could still do if his pride allowed him to. Lollobrigida, about to break out of another act in the same circus, makes a play for the Curtis character in order to join his act, along with Lancaster (and against his wishes).

The Rainmaker was the result of another Hal Wallis buy from Broadway, and of a compromise with Burt. The producer had planned from the first to star Katharine Hepburn as the Kansas spinster Lizzie, who is brought to life by the roving supersalesman of the title. Lancaster, meanwhile, was resisting Wallis's attempts to get him to play Wyatt Earp opposite Kirk Douglas's Doc Holliday in *Gunfight at the OK Corral*. 'Burt telephoned me in the middle of the night,' Wallis recalled, 'to say that if I would let him play Starbuck, the lead in *The Rainmaker*, he would do *Gunfight at the OK Corral*, and that would take care of our two remaining commitments. I agreed and they were two of Burt's best pictures.'

Lancaster was given first billing in *The Rainmaker*, because Hepburn had been away from Hollywood for four years and had lost a lot of her star power. N. Richard Nash was hired to do the adaptation of his own play (which was turned into a hit Broadway musical in 1962, starring Robert Horton and Inga Swenson). The Rainmaker is essentially a charlatan itinerent peddlar and medicine man who arrives at the Curry family farm during an especially dry, hot summer, claiming he can bring rain upon the parched land for $100. Rain does come, and with it a new confidence in the Currys, particularly Lizzie. Under Joseph Anthony's direction, both Lancaster as Starbuck and Hepburn as Lizzie gave beautifully believable performances. For Lancaster, the con-man character was a portent of *Elmer Gantry*.

'Some people feel there is a similarity between Starbuck and Elmer Gantry,' Lancaster said. 'In a way, I suppose there is – at least in their vitality. But Elmer was basically a fraud whereas Starbuck – for all his bravado – was really insecure. He's the one who is the flawed person, whereas Lizzie is the strong person.'

Wallis remembered Lancaster being 'late on the set the first day. Kate is intolerant of unprofessional behaviour, and she gave him hell. She walked into the centre of the sound stage and said: "I'm here, all these people are here, and if you're not going to be here on time we can't work." He learned his lesson and was on time for the rest of the shooting.'

While Lancaster worked on *The Rainmaker*, his production company produced *The Bachelor Party*, another Paddy Chayefsky adaptation of one of his television plays to the large screen. Like *Marty*, *The Bachelor Party* was about ordinary urban people, specifically a young husband, played ably by Don Murray, who attends his pre-marriage stag affair on the day he also finds out he is to be a father. He feels increasingly trapped by his situation the more his friends try to entertain him. The picture, done for three times the budget of *Marty*, was a critical success. It also earned the late Carolyn Jones, playing a sad goodtime girl, an Academy Award nomination as best supporting actress. But its minimal box office, as Harold Hecht noted, caused its investors to 'come a cropper because they thought they'd have another *Marty*, including ourselves. *Marty* was peculiar unto itself.'

Despite his initial reluctance to undertake it, *Gunfight at the OK Corral* proved to be a good career move, if only to solidify the 'good guy' side of Lancaster's movie reputation. 'I was wise enough to realise that audiences put a label on you,' he noted, 'and mine had a big hat and spurs written on it. So I made a Western every three or four movies, hoping that if they liked me at the *OK Corral* they'd come and see the offbeat ones. I think the system worked; certainly it worked for me. I don't despise the Westerns I've made – some have been great entertainment – but no man can keep his self-respect if he's always chasing Injuns.'

The Wyatt Earp-Doc Holliday story, which culminated in the celebrated shoot-out at Tombstone, Arizona on 26 October 1881, had been filmed several times before, most notably in John Ford's *My Darling Clementine*, with Henry Fonda and Victor Mature. But Wallis said he wanted to do *Gunfight at the OK Corral* in more realistic, less romantic fashion than its predecessors. He hired Leon Uris to do the script, and director John Sturges, 'whose *Bad Day at Black Rock* with Spencer Tracy had just the gritty quality I wanted in *Gunfight*', said Wallis. The producer, a major collector of Frederic

Remington paintings, requested 'the burned out brown look of a Remington' from cameraman Charles Lang, Jnr. Those were the easy parts.

Lancaster and Douglas were indeed ideal casting as Dodge City's Marshal Wyatt Earp and the charming killer Doc Holliday, but in the ten years since Wallis had first teamed them in *I Walk Alone*, both had become major box office stars and powerful producer-actors. Sheilah Graham reported that they came back to Wallis 'for a hundred times what he had paid them before; this time they were in the driver's seat and they made sure Wallis knew it.'

'From the start, both stars asserted themselves,' said Wallis. 'They reminded us constantly that they were directors as well as actors and tried to override Sturges, but John was a match for them. They rewrote their dialogue at night, but this was an exercise in futility, as I insisted that the lines be read exactly as Leon Uris had written them. Burt finally exploded, demanding that John let him play a scene his way, with dialogue he had written. It was totally unrelated to the action, but John humoured him. Burt played the scene to the hilt, shouting himself hoarse. The speech was out of his system. The film was also out of the camera.'

The Vista-Vision and Technicolor production was shot on location in Arizona. Uris emphasised the strong bond of mutual respect that developed between Earp and Holliday, but he did flesh out the bare facts with frequent scenes including frontier ladies Rhonda Fleming and Jo Van Fleet, who was particularly memorable as Holliday's woman. Earp was portrayed as sadly regretful of the violence in his line of work, and Holliday, although a consumptive bigot, was also seen as self-reproachful.

The gunfight scene itself was 'choreographed like a

ballet', according to Wallis. 'John and I drew up a map plotting every move Burt and Kirk and the Clanton boys made. We asked the actors to play the scene deadpan. We assumed Western men engaged in struggles to the death didn't show emotion: they accepted the rule of the bullet and didn't question it. I asked Burt to be especially careful about playing deadpan. In answer to his question, 'What should I be thinking about when I'm in the gunfight?' John and I replied simultaneously, 'Meanwhile, back at the ranch.' He listened and played the scene perfectly.

Douglas and Lancaster preferred to remember only happy times on the set of *Gunfight at the OK Corral*. 'We were both alone, and we spent weeks together on location,' Burt recalled in 1983. 'We shared adjoining rooms at the hotel. We'd sit up most of the night discussing our families, our children, our careers, our hopes, our dreams – and it was there that our friendship ripened.'

But Lancaster's streak of cruelty even toward those he loved best surfaced at least once during *Gunfight at the OK Corral*. As he and Douglas were walking off the set after filming a scene, a crowd of autograph seekers surrounded Burt. 'Why don't you ask Mr Douglas for his?' he snarled. 'Great performer. Of course, you don't recognise him without his built–up shoes.' By the time the two actors reached their automobiles, Douglas was weeping.

Lancaster's next movie was his most 'offbeat' ever: *Sweet Smell of Success*, in which he played (for the first time in eyeglasses) the evil and corrupt Broadway columnist J. J. Hunsecker. The movie was produced by James Hill, who was promoted from story editor and made a full partner of the company, which changed its name to Hecht-Hill-Lancaster for *Sweet Smell of Success*.

'It was the greatest failure our company ever made,' Burt recalled. 'We lost a fortune on it, but it has become a critic's darling over the years. Not enough moviegoers cared for it. I don't think they understood the background, the rather strange Clifford Odets dialogue. Tony Curtis was absolutely marvellous – it's the best thing he's ever done, I think. It should have won him the Academy Award.'

Sweet Smell of Success was not a simple film to make. Lancaster not only fought with British director Alexander MacKendrick, who was making his first American movie, but almost came to blows with Odets, who had written the screenplay with Ernest Lehman from Lehman's novelette of the same name. Odets and Lancaster were having a seemingly pleasant lunch one day during production, when Burt snapped, 'I've got a good mind to beat you up.' 'Why?' inquired the startled Odets. 'I think you could have written some of the scenes better,' shouted Lancaster. 'Go ahead, beat me up,' said the stunned playwright, 'I'd like to get my hands on some of your money.'

'Sandy' MacKendrick, on the other hand, according to Lancaster, 'couldn't make up his mind. He'd set up shots on the soundstage for a scene that would play six minutes. There would be thirty-five camera moves on a dolly. The whole floor was taped. We had to hit marks like crazy. The camera moved continuously – into close-ups, pulling back, shooting over here to this person. Move in, turn. We rehearsed all day, until four in the afternoon, just to get the technical part down. The head grip and the rest of the crew were sweating, knowing that if they missed one mark, the shot would be ruined. But we did it, clicked it all off. Sandy called: "Cut. Print." Then he'd stop, waiting. I'd say, "Something the matter, Sandy?" "No, it went fine, you all did it fine, only . . . let's do one more." So we went through it again. Again, fine. Cut. I was delighted. We had six minutes of film, a good day's work – and done in the most interesting style. But he still wouldn't be satisfied. He'd shake his head and say, "I don't like it, we've got to change it – change everything." Well, you put up with it because you put up with Babe Ruth even if he's drunk. We respected Sandy; he was a little kooky, but he was good. He did a marvellous job. It wasn't his fault the picture lost money.'

MacKendrick and Lancaster may have had their differences in picture-making style, but the director was unabashed in his admiration of the star's presence and potential. 'Burt has never faltered in his career,' said MacKendrick. 'One of the things he has, that the stars had, is that he can walk into a room and there is a change in the heartbeat. If you had some instrument you could measure it. It's like having a wild animal there suddenly. It has to do with aggression and potential violence. I think some politicians have it, but no English actor. I was very conscious that here was an ego different to others. The stars had this neurosis which goes right to the edge. You have somehow to use this to get performances from these deep-sea monsters. There was this enormous difference between him and Tony Curtis. Tony has a fantastic vanity, but no ego. He could act Burt off the screen, but he will never be a star. He hasn't this granite quality of the ego.'

Sweet Smell of Success was dark and uncompromising in its depiction of the seamier side of Broadway life. Lancaster as Hunsecker was malicious and amoral in the use of his power as a columnist to manipulate sleazy press agents, political figures and show business aspirants. Tony Curtis was cast against his glamour boy image as a weaselly hustler-promoter and showed for the first time an extraordinary acting ability. Susan Harrison played the younger sister of Hunsecker, the one person he professes to love and wants to protect from her fiancé, whom he deems unsuitable.

Hill said of the failure of *Sweet Smell of Success*, 'People kept waiting to see Burt jump out of a tree.' Hecht said he hated the picture and wished it had never been made.

To counteract the commercial failure of *Sweet Smell of Success*, Hecht-Hill-Lancaster followed it with a calculated crowd-pleaser: *Run Silent, Run Deep*, a story about the submarine service based on a novel by Captain Edward L. Beach. Lancaster's business judgment easily outweighed his vanity, so his company signed Clark Gable and gave him top billing. Robert Wise was hired to direct, and Captain Beach to serve as technical adviser. Graphic action in the submarine and the effect of those cramped quarters on the men took precedence over plot. Gable was a surviving commander whose submarine was sunk by a Japanese destroyer in the Bongo Straits in 1942. He becomes obsessed with catching and sinking that exact enemy ship. Given command of another submarine whose well-liked executive officer (Lancaster) had expected to take over, Gable at first encounters a hostile crew. He gradually wins them over and they support his efforts at revenge. When he gets his chance to attack the Japanese vessel, Gable must ignore his orders to do it. The destroyer is sunk, the submarine surfaces to be attacked by enemy aircraft, during which attack Gable is wounded fatally.

Gable was fifty-seven at the the time of *Run Silent, Run Deep*, and Lancaster was forty-five but, as usual, looking considerably younger. He was perfectly cast as a man who, in second position, has to restrain his anger, and he suffered nothing at all by being second-billed to Clark Gable. Bosley Crowther in *The New York Times* said of *Run Silent, Run Deep:* 'A better film about guys in "the silent service" has not been made.'

* * * * * *

'I am terribly wealthy,' Lancaster announced in the middle of 1958. I am worth three and a half million dollars. I have five children. I've got everything I want. What more could I possibly need? I am not moved by the desire to make more money or win more fame. I've got enough of both and there comes a time when you can't get any more of either. I am just interested in doing things that interest me. When I first started in movies I was unsure of myself, and insecure. I would flare up easily. When success comes as quickly as it came to me there are bound to be problems. You ask yourself, "how do I come to be here and have I any right to be here?" It took me a certain amount of time to adjust. Now I think I'm adjusted. I keep calm.'

CHAPTER EIGHT

Elmer Gantry and Oscar

IN 1958 Hecht-Hill-Lancaster bought the movie rights to Terence Rattigan's London and New York stage success *Separate Tables* and hired Laurence Olivier to direct as well as to star in the leading male role of the bogus major. Olivier's then-wife Vivien Leigh was set to play the part of the estranged wife of an alcoholic writer who has followed him to an English seaside inn, in the hope of a reconciliation. On stage, *Separate Tables* consisted of two distinct but related acts, both set in the hotel, each telling a sort of love story. An actor (Eric Portman) and actress (Margaret Leighton) played the two central roles in each half. On screen this tech-nique could not work, so Rattigan agreed to intermingle the stories, on the condition that he write the screen-play, and the consequent necessity for four starring roles. Lancaster was set to play the writer, whose nationality was changed to American, and his co-star in *From Here to Eternity*, Deborah Kerr, was picked to play the repressed mother-dominated spinster who is attracted to 'the major'. Gladys Cooper played the mother and Wendy Hiller, the manageress of the hotel, with whom the Lancaster character has been having an affair.

But trouble between Lancaster and Olivier started on the first day of rehearsals for *Separate Tables*. Burt was used to arguing with his directors over the conception of his role, but Olivier was not used to being argued with. Since Lancaster was also the producer, Olivier felt he had no course but to resign both as director and leading actor. Vivien Leigh quit with him. David Niven was brought in to play the major, and Rita Hayworth, who was then married to James Hill, was granted her wish to play Lancaster's estranged wife. Delbert Mann, who had directed *Marty*, was hired to replace Olivier as director of *Separate Tables*.

Niven and Kerr dominate the film version of *Separate Tables*, and Niven won the Best Actor Oscar for 1958 for his touching portrayal of the disgraced but forgiven fraud. Kerr was nominated as Best Actress for the fourth of six times without winning, and Hiller won the Best Supporting Actress Award. Lancaster and Hayworth were out of place as Americans in this particular English story, and out of the running, although many critics considered *Separate Tables* to be Hayworth's finest work on screen. She cherished Margaret Leighton's appraisal, relayed through husband Jim Hill: 'If I could have done the part in the theatre as well as your wife did it on the screen, they'd never have had her take my place.'

The Devil's Disciple, George Bernard Shaw's 1897 play about the American Revolution, was even in Shaw's opinion far from his best play, but Lancaster and Kirk Douglas were both so eager to do it as a movie that they joined forces as co-producers as well as co-stars. Douglas took the title role, a rascal named Richard

[104]

Dudgeon. Lancaster played a stern village minister, the Reverend Anderson, a religious pacifist who joins in the American fight for Independence, and at one point emerges victorious in combat against a group of British soldiers. Burt wanted Laurence Olivier as the British Commander, General John ('Gentleman Johnny') Burgoyne badly enough to patch up their differences. Olivier has the few good lines (like 'Martyrdom, sir, is the only way in which a man can become famous without ability') and is the only memorable player in this otherwise turgid movie. Although adaptors Roland Kibbee and John Dighton had rewritten Shaw's play considerably, they were abetted by Douglas and Lancaster.

'We had to pay $600,000 to Shaw's estate for the property,' Burt recalled. 'We couldn't get a script we wanted. Finally we had to shelve it for a while. Then Kirk dropped by one day to say that he was interested in the Dick Dudgeon role. Originally, I was going to play that role with Monty Clift playing the minister. That didn't work out for rather sad reasons. Because of Clift's problems at the time, United Artists couldn't get a company to insure him. But Kirk started it up again. We had at first planned to make it a three million dollar colour film. Now it was going to be a black and white movie that cost a million and a half, a very limited budget. The only one who got any money out of it was Olivier, who got somewhere between $150,000 and $200,000 for playing the general.'

The Devil's Disciple was filmed in England, where it had more than script problems. Alexander MacKendrick, who had been hired to direct, despite his difference of style with Lancaster on *Sweet Smell of Success*, was fired after the first week, and replaced by Guy Hamilton. 'I explained to Sandy that because so much

[105]

of our limited budget had gone toward purchasing the property, we had a forty-eight-day shooting schedule,' said Lancaster. 'Every day we went over, Harold and I would have to reach down in our pockets and Harold assured him we weren't about to do that. Sandy told us not to worry, but after shooting a week he had only two days of film. So we called him in and let him go. It's ironic that his two days of the film are the best in the picture. But we did what we had to do. It was that cut and dried. The English press ran a bunch of articles about what bad fellows we were. But that was the deal and Sandy knew it.'

The resulting picture was neither a critical nor a commercial success. Hollis Alpert in *The Saturday Review* said that Douglas and Lancaster suffered in the shadow of Olivier, and *Time* complained that 'Actor Lancaster glooms away Shaw's most romantic scenes as if he were lost on a Bronte moor.'

Even less likely to be commercial was Lancaster's company's next movie, *Take a Giant Step*, in which he did not appear. It was based on a Broadway play of the same name by Louis S. Peterson about a black youth (Johnny Nash, later better known as a pop singer) growing up in a small New England town unused to Negroes. Its social conscience was commendable as was its casting, including Ruby Dee and Beah Richards. But in 1959–60 it failed to get sufficient bookings to make money, and critical opinion was divided. While *The Saturday Review's* Arthur Knight said, 'No film to date, not even *The Defiant Ones*, has attempted to describe so explicitly what it means to be a Negro in a white man's world', *Variety* called it 'well-intended but not so well-made', and *The New York Times* described it as 'a cross between a social justice brochure and a Negro Andy Hardy film'.

MGM decided to invest at least fifteen million dollars in a re-make of the silent movie *Ben-Hur*, for a 1959 release. As box office insurance they wanted an established star who seemed sufficiently at home in costume drama and who was athletic enough to race chariots. Lancaster was the studio's obvious choice for the Technicolor wide-screen spectacle, despite his recent penchant for little pictures that did little business. MGM offered him a million dollars to star in *Ben-Hur*, but Burt, objecting to the story's strongly Christian ethos, declined the role. 'I grew up in the slums of New York, among Jews, Negroes, Italians, East Indians, Catholics, Protestants, Buddhists, all faiths, all colours,' he said. 'So how could I convincingly portray the idea that Christianity is the one true faith?' Charlton Heston, who was to have played Lancaster's rival, Messal, was switched to the star part. He won the chariot race and a Best Actor Academy Award. *Ben-Hur* won a total of eleven Oscars in 1959, the most ever received by a single motion picture.

In 1960, James Hill produced *The Unforgiven*, further proof that Lancaster intended to pursue his interest in social issues in his movies. John Huston directed this anti-bigotry Western set in the Texas Panhandle in the late 1860s, but shot on location in Durango, Mexico. Lancaster played the foster brother of Audrey Hepburn, an unlikely choice of actress to portray a full-blooded Kiowa Indian, albeit one who grew up thinking she was white. The tribe arrives at the family doorstep one day to reclaim her – or attack. Lancaster's character refuses to return her to the Indians, angering both them and the whites who want to give her back to avoid trouble. The subsequent battles are savage and prolonged, ending in the defeat of the Indians. Once it is clear that they are no blood kin, Hepburn and

Lancaster are free to marry and of necessity fight racial prejudice for the rest of their lives. Each of the stars received $300,000 for *The Unforgiven*, which had a hefty budget for a 1960 movie filmed in Mexico of five million dollars.

Huston called his making *The Unforgiven* 'a mistake. Some of my pictures I don't care for, but *The Unforgiven* is the only one I actually dislike. Hecht-Hill-Lancaster had come to me with the proposal. I read the script by Ben Maddow (who had worked with me on *The Asphalt Jungle*), considered the strength of the cast – Burt Lancaster, Audrey Hepburn, Audie Murphy, Charles Bickford and Lillian Gish – and decided to do it. I thought I saw in Maddow's script the potential for a more serious – and better – film than either he or Hecht-Hill-Lancaster had originally contemplated; I wanted to turn it into the story of racial intolerance in the frontier town, a comment on the real nature of community morality. The trouble was that the producers disagreed. What they wanted was what I had unfortunately signed on to make when I accepted the job in the first place – a swashbuckler about a larger-than-life frontiersman. The difference of intention did not become an issue until we were very close to shooting time, and quite mistakenly I agreed to stick it out, thus violating my own conviction that a picture-maker should undertake nothing but what he believes in – regardless. From that moment the entire picture turned sour. It was as if some celestial vengeance had been loosed upon me for infidelity to my principles.'

Audrey Hepburn, a novice rider, fell off a horse, fracturing a vertebra which delayed filming for three weeks. 'I felt responsible,' Huston remembered, 'having put her on a horse for the first time.' Murphy and a friend of Huston's who had gone duck hunting together on a lake in Durango, almost drowned. Murphy's hip was wounded in World War II and he couldn't swim, and the friend tried to save him. Inge Morath, a photographer and championship swimmer, spied the pair through her telephoto lens, stripped to her bra and panties and swam out to save them.

But the worst thing that happened to Burt during *The Unforgiven* occurred at the opening of a new country club outside Durango. He and several other international celebrities were playing in its first major golf tournament, when Huston and another friend flew over in a small rented airplane and dropped 2000 ping-pong balls on the fairway. 'We inscribed them with the most terrible things we could think of,' Huston recalled. "Go home you Yankee sons of bitches!" "Fuck you dirty Mexican cabrones!" and similar sentiments. It was a triumph. Nobody could possibly locate a golf ball. It took days to clean up the course, the tournament was cancelled and everybody was furious – especially Burt Lancaster, who was one of the tournament sponsors and took his golf quite seriously.'

Lancaster's only terse recollection of *The Unforgiven* and Huston was, 'John's a charming man, but he takes chances with the safety of his actors.'

Elmer Gantry, Lancaster felt, 'was something special. Dick Brooks and I worked for seven months on the script. I had got to know him fairly well back in 1947 when he wrote *Brute Force*, then we went our separate ways and didn't bump into each other for years. When we did, maybe five years before we made *Elmer Gantry*, it was at the race-track. He asked me if I knew anything about *Elmer Gantry* and I answered that I was familiar with the Sinclair Lewis book. He said, "I think I'm going to get the property." I told him I thought it would make a wonderful movie, and we parted and that was that. A year later I ran into him again at a restaurant near Paramount where he was having lunch. He said, "I've got the property; we have to do the movie someday." I told him that would be fine and said goodbye. Dissolve. Two more years go by. I get a call from Dick: "I'm going to Europe for four months and I'm going to write *Elmer Gantry*." I still wasn't taking him too seriously, but six months later he sent me the script.

'I didn't care for it; it was terribly long, followed the book in detail. I phoned him and we got into a violent argument about it. I told him, "If you really want to do this, I'm with you. But don't start the movie with me as a twenty-year-old kid in a seminary – that's not gonna play; let's start the film later on." He gulped. For a while he wouldn't talk to me. Then his agent called and we went back together. Dick said, "I hear you play a lot of golf." I told him that was correct. "Well there's no time for that, no more golf. Instead you come over to the studio every day and work with me on this script." For seven months we did that. But everything, that and the preparation, was worth it. *Elmer Gantry* was a labour of love.'

Lancaster felt that 'Sinclair Lewis wrote Elmer Gantry as a caricature; he made him so one-sided and so bad that it was hard to identify with him. He never loved his wife. He never cared about any other human being in the world, yet he felt comfortable in the area of religiosity. Swaying people's emotions excited him. With Dick Brooks I felt that an audience had to recognise something human in him. So we had him interested in dames and drinking, as well as hollering hellfire and brimstone. We weren't trying to uglify him, we were merely trying to make him a recognisable, full-blooded human being with common weaknesses and vanities.

'Gantry was essentially a ham', said Lancaster. 'He liked having his voice stir up excitement. He was a supersalesman, a hail-fellow-well-met type; he wanted the boys to like him. In a sense we were trying to say that this man was looking for something, and in the process of looking for it he wanted somebody to be with him and reassure him.' Thus in the film version, Gantry is not even an ordained minister as he is in the novel. Rather, he is a travelling salesman and a former divinity student who was expelled for seducing a deacon's daughter. He is first seen as a saloon patron in a small southern town, who takes pity on two female Salvation Army members trying to solicit Christmas donations. Gantry sermonises to his fellow gambling drinkers and extracts money from them, which he hands over to the girls. He then becomes fascinated by Sister Sharon Falconer (Jean Simmons), a tent meeting revivalist, first charming his way into her circle, then becoming a fiery preacher himself. A prostitute (Shirley Jones) that Gantry had deflowered, frames him and manages to turn his public against him. When Jones admits she lied about him, Gantry is restored to the Falconer crusade and public favour. When a fire kills Sister Sharon, the con man will clearly carry on her salvationist efforts.

Brooks described *Elmer Gantry* as 'the story of a man who wants what everyone is supposed to want – money, sex, religion. He's the All-American boy.'

'It was the easiest role I was ever given to play because I was, in essence, playing myself,' Lancaster said. 'Some parts you fall into like an old glove. *Elmer* wasn't really acting – that was me. But I used John

[111]

Huston as my model for the role – his mannerisms, the charming demeanour he has.'

'Lancaster pulls out virtually all the stops . . . to create a memorable characterisation,' wrote *Variety* on the release of *Elmer Gantry*. A. H. Weiler, in *The New York Times*, said, 'Without the performance of Burt Lancaster the film's overall effect would be vitiated. He is an Elmer Gantry who would have delighted the cold, inquiring eye and crusading soul of Sinclair Lewis.' 'He *is* Gantry,' agreed Arthur Knight in *The Saturday Review*, 'from the flashy suit right down to the holes in his socks.'

Winning his second New York Film Critics Award for *Elmer Gantry* made Lancaster a favourite to win an Academy Award as Best Actor of 1960. Lancaster admitted, 'I'd like to win it.' His competition was formidable: Olivier in *The Entertainer*, Jack Lemmon in *The Apartment*, Trevor Howard in *Sons and Lovers* and Spencer Tracy in *Inherit the Wind*. Lancaster felt that the New York Critics had 'high standards; consequently when they give you an award of this kind, you feel that they are expressing a considered opinion. You don't have to feel that politics is involved. When Hollywood gives out its Oscars, you generally feel that there is a political manoeuvering going on. So in my opinion – and I think all Hollywood actors really feel this way – the New York Critics award is the prestige award, even though it doesn't carry the box office weight of an Oscar. I wish I had more enthusiasm for winning it. Winning will represent a kind of popular victory, but I doubt if it's as fair a test as it ought to be. The decision on Best Actor should come from the actors alone; another actor can recognise craft and style. He is less likely to be motivated by personal likes or dislikes, although emotion may colour his decision. People in the motion picture industry are sentimental. If you've been nominated before, your previous nominations have something to do with your chances. That doesn't make winning less rewarding, but it does make it another kind of reward.'

Lancaster won the Best Actor Award for *Elmer Gantry*, only his second nomination, kidding backstage that he was accepting it 'in the name of Stuart Chase', which had almost been his *nom de thesp*. Lancaster also took satisfaction in Brooks's Academy Award for Best Screenplay. Shirley Jones, in her first serious dramatic role, won the Best Supporting Actress Award.

An Oscar-winning actor can always have his choice of roles in his next venture. Lancaster's social conscience led him and Hecht-Hill-Lancaster to choose *The Young Savages*, a story of juvenile delinquency in Spanish Harlem, Burt's old neighbourhood, which had undergone a drastic change in the years he'd been gone. John Frankenheimer, a well-known 'live television' director who was launching a feature career that, among other things, would emphasise location filming rather than movie studio sets and backlots, was hired. Sidney Pollack was brought to California by Frankenheimer to be the movie's dialogue director, and to coach three kids with almost no acting experience, but important roles in *The Young Savages*. 'Lancaster and I became friendly on the set,' Pollack recalled, 'and he pushed me over into direction. He called Universal Studios to see if they had a training programme. They had none, but agreed to let me observe for six months; at the end of that time they would decide whether or not to take a chance on letting me direct a [television] show.' Pollack passed his internship and went on direct Lancaster in *The Scalphunters* and *Castle Keep* and to work on *The Leopard* and *The Swimmer*.

The Young Savages, which was based on the Evan Hunter novel, *A Matter of Conviction,* was shot in East Harlem. Lancaster played an ambitious assistant district attorney who himself had grown up in a slum. Ordered to investigate the murder of a Puerto Rican street gang member, presumably by three of his compatriots, as quickly as possible, the Lancaster character finds the case not so simple. His reservations bring down the wrath of his superior and the neighbourhood's citizens, endangering his life and that of his wife (Dina Merrill). But at the trial he is proved right.

'I don't think anybody is better with the camera than John Frankenheimer,' said Lancaster. 'Those early *Playhouse 90s* that he directed weren't just interesting plays, they were shot uniquely, were sometimes even crazy and bizarre. At the outset of *The Young Savages* John and I had some problems, I felt his approach to his work did not get the best results because of his attitude. He was tough and arrogant and terribly demanding on the set, sometimes to his own detriment. After we settled our personal problems we got along great, became great friends. I did five movies with him.'

Playhouse 90 also provided the impetus for Lancaster's next movie, Stanley Kramer's all-star production of *Judgment at Nuremberg.* Abby Mann wrote the screenplay from his own television original, and Kramer chose to make it more than twice as long (189 minutes) as the teleplay. Kramer filmed much of the movie detailing the 1948 war crimes trial of four Nazi judges in actual German locations, and incorporated footage of Nazi atrocities. As the principal defendant, Ernst Janning (played by Paul Lukas on television), Lancaster employed a German accent and ageing make-up. Janning sits impassively through most of the long trial, not attempting to defend himself. He does request a private meeting with the American presiding judge (Spencer Tracy), in which he says, 'Those millions of people . . . I never knew it would come to that.' The American judge replied, 'Herr Janning, it came to you the first time you sentenced a man to death you knew to be innocent.' When it becomes clear that the trial is dragging on without a likely resolution, Janning wearily rises to denounce himself and the German judicial system during the Nazi regime: 'It is not easy to tell the truth, but if there is to be any salvation for Germany, we who knew her guilt must admit it, whatever the pain or humiliation. My counsel would have you believe we were not aware of the concentration camps. Where were we? If we didn't know the details, it was because we didn't want to know.'

The eight-minute admission, which enfolds the guilt of his three co-defendants to a lesser degree, settles the trial, to their disgust and that of their defence attorney, Maximilian Schell, who won the Best Actor Oscar for 1961 for his work in *Judgment at Nuremberg*. Tracy was nominated for the same award, Judy Garland was nominated for Best Supporting Actress, and Montgomery Clift for Best Supporting Actor for their performances as victims of Nazi torture. Mann won the Academy Award for Best Screenplay. Most critics found the casting, which also included Marlene Dietrich and Richard Widmark, impeccable even if recognisable faces distracted from the seriousness of the subject matter. But few, especially those who had seen Lukas in the part, liked Lancaster as Janning.

Lancaster had also failed to endear himself to the cast of *Judgment at Nuremberg*. Although he was not the producer of the picture, merely a hired actor, Burt tried his usual trick of taking over some of the direction. He and Schell got into a terrible argument when Lancaster accused Schell of having missed an important cue. Schell not only denied having done so, he challenged Lancaster to look at the dailies to prove the point. 'This is a most unprofessional attitude,' Lancaster screamed. But when the rushes were viewed, Schell was right.

CHAPTER NINE

Birdman of Alcatraz

IN THE AUTUMN of 1961 the disastrous Bel-Air fire destroyed 456 homes in that exclusive area of Los Angeles, including that of the Lancasters. The damage done by the canyon country conflagration was virtually all to property and not to people, prompting Associated Press correspondent James Bacon to observe, 'It was an unusual fire – no refugees in Red Cross shelters. Most of those burned out checked into the Beverly Hills Hotel. It was probably the wealthiest group of refugees since the Bolsheviks drove the Czar and the Imperial household out of St Petersburg.' At six o'clock in the morning after the fire, the lobby of the hotel was crowded with many homeless movie stars, Burt among them, with his ten-year-old daughter Joanna.

'The kids want me to rebuild it stone by stone,' he said of their totally destroyed residence, then worth an estimated half a million dollars, 'and I guess I will.' Fortunately, some $250,000 worth of his finest paintings had been lent to the Los Angeles County Art Museum the week before the fire, and were safe. 'So many other people were affected by it that I couldn't feel particularly sorry for myself,' Lancaster said. 'It was just something that happened to all of us. The only things of real importance that I lost were pictures of the children when they were kids.'

Lancaster's family had been growing steadily, with the birth of daughters Susan Elizabeth, in July 1949, Joanna in July 1951 and Sighle (pronounced Sheilah) in July 1954. With sons James Stephen having been born in July 1946, and William Henry in November 1947, and his own birthday on 2 November (which he proudly noted was the same as Luchino Visconti's), Lancaster said, 'July and November are the birthday months in our house.'

Expansion and remodelling of the Bel-Air house had begun with the arrival of Susan, and by the time Joanna came along, the value of the Lancaster spread was an estimated $300,000, with a full-sized baseball diamond, on an acre-and-a–half tract below the house, floodlit at night, where Burt coached both his boys and his girls, to help keep them at home. Remembering the abundance of activity available to him as a child in East Harlem, Burt bitched, 'Where we live there is nothing for the kids to do, but go to a movie, and then we have to drive them because it's too far to go on foot and there is no safe place for them to walk. So it really isn't as good for children as it might seem.'

The kind of father who frequently packed up all five children and took them on a camping trip (feeding and dressing the younger girls), Lancaster also believed in talking to them as if they were adults. And in case any of them had inborn acrobatic instincts he taught each of the kids to walk on his or her hands at an early age. The children often visited him at the studio, and the four oldest had travelled with him and Norma to locations in Italy, the Fiji Islands and Mexico. Sighle came along just in time to join the rest of the family in France for the filming of *Trapeze*.

In spite of his own fear of water, Lancaster had built a huge swimming pool in 1950, when second son William Henry was three and contracted polio and needed the therapeutic benefits of swimming. Billy had several operations but walked with a limp until he had another operation at age sixteen, when he achieved full growth in the lower part of his body. In 1961 William and his older brother James had their own wing in the Bel-Air house, while the sisters simply had a suite each. Paintings by Renoir, Utrillo, Vlaminck and Chagall hung everywhere in the house until the fortunate loan just before the fire – a testimony both to the teaching of David Morrison back at the Union Settlement House, and to the resounding success of *Trapeze*, *Vera Cruz*, *Marty* and *Separate Tables*. The previous Christmas Lancaster had startled his agent with the gift of a Utrillo, walking into the office with the unwrapped painting under his arm like a morning newspaper or a new script.

At the Hecht-Hill-Lancaster offices at the Goldwyn Studios, things appeared to be going equally swimmingly. The only minor thorn was that Samuel Goldwyn refused to let Burt paint the offices, which had been a large prop warehouse, a bright barn red. 'It would ruin the look of my studio,' said Sam of the complex, which was a soft sand colour. Burt lost the war but was allowed a victory in one battle: he got to put up red shutters. Hecht-Hill-Lancaster attempted to get into the growing television business by producing a pilot programme based on *The Bachelor Party*, entitled *The Office*. It didn't sell to a network and the producers went back to what they knew best – making movies.

Hecht-Hill-Lancaster was about to embark on the last of six productions to be released by United Artists under the terms of a twenty-six million dollar deal. Lancaster was proud of Hecht-Hill-Lancaster's unique contributions to independent production. 'I've always respected the work of writers, because everything starts there,' he said. 'We were the first to insist that the writers be on the set while we made the picture. We couldn't afford to pay them their full salary, but they went along with it because nobody had ever given them the chance before to be there to see that nobody hacked up their scripts.

'We used Broadway actors in secondary roles. The typical thing in those days was to use Beautiful People only. Of course, if you were making romantic fluff by, let's say, Kathleen Norris, naturally the characters would be *papier maché*. But if you were doing something about real people, we figured, why not use real people?'

Lancaster was equally proud that Hecht-Hill-Lancaster had been able to get top talent like Gary Cooper and Sir Carol Reed to work for them when even the biggest studios could not. 'We cut them in on the profits,' he explained of what was then brand new but would become common practice in the film industry. 'There's an extra dimension to a man's work when he knows he owns a part of it. There is no profit to anyone turning out a bad picture. The old days of paying a flat fee to fine actors and directors have gone the way of the dodo bird. You can't attract the best talent that way. Talented people deserve a break; they've earned the right to share in the profits. There are plenty of good, capable, directors around town who will give you exactly what is written in the script and no more.

But a man like Carol Reed gives you something plus in imagination.'

Hecht and Lancaster, having been together longer, had more frequent disagreements than either had with Hill. Hecht maintained that Burt still regarded acting as 'sissy' stuff and spent so much time on the business side of movies because it made him feel more manly. Hill was a bit in awe of both Harold and Burt, for different reasons: 'Among Harold's many talents, the one that particularly interested me was his ability to pull the rug out from under a person. It was the subtlety with which he managed this that was impressive, because he invariably won the admiration of the other party even as they were picking themselves up off the floor.

'On the other hand,' Hill added, 'Burt never got his exercise that way. When it came to conditioning, he spent most of his time running or working out on the parallel bars. But what set him apart was an aspect of his character I'd discovered on the golf course. We were at the Riviera Golf Club on the second hole. I had just putted out. While I was still reaching into the cup for my ball, Burt said, "What did you take?" He always said it with the steely blue-eyed gaze, the one that could empty out any bar – even the OK Corral. Before I could answer, he told me, "You took an eight."

'In accomplishing that eight, I had hooked my drive into the trees, then moved deeper into the woods on my next shot, and finally into a trap. The lip on the trap had been so high there was no way to see over it or into it. So after taking three more to get out of there, I had to heft a high wedge over another clump of trees, and found myself on the green. That was the first time we had seen one another since leaving the tee. Once the other two players in our foursome had arrived on the green, too, I managed a fifty-foot putt – and sunk it. If something congratulatory had been said about that first, I might not have been so engrossed in shaving a stroke off my score while lost in the rough, and another two when I was hidden from view in that trap. Instead, it was only natural to hesitate when I heard, "What did you take?"

'That rattled me sufficiently that I decided to knock off only one of those strokes in the trap.But before I was able to total my score, Burt not only told me what it was but ticked off each of the eight shots I had made. Then he did something even more incredible. He told each of the other two players exactly how many strokes they had taken. It never entered my mind to question where he found the time to hit his own ball. Nor did I ever think to question his score.

'There was another problem with having Burt as a friend – he could not only remember your every stroke on the golf course, but just about everything you said off it...I mean, when you talk about someone who has everything, including the ability to walk around on his fingertips, that's Burt.'

Hill and Hecht even went along with Lancaster when he decided to get the new mouth that made his grin so distinctive. A California dentist had pioneered a theory of the perfect bite: a person's mouth could be remodelled so that the two sets of teeth did not grind against each other, and therefore no fillings would be needed subsequently. Burt bought the treatment for about $10,000, and his two partners, to save him any embarrassment, did the same. Meeting all three partners in Hecht-Hill-Lancaster at once to talk business became a dazzling experience in more ways than one.

Lancaster used his new teeth to lash out not only at directors, but also at his bridge partners and his business partner, 'Lord Mole', with a temper that was becoming legendary. Burt was invited to a party to show off Hecht's expensively furbished new home. He naturally didn't want to go to a cocktail party but was persuaded that it would look bad if he stayed away. He had a drink or two, and was observed to be in a dark mood. 'Where is the can?' he shouted. Receiving no answer, he persisted in his tantrum: 'How do you like this? He builds this dump with my money and I don't even know where the can is.' Hecht hurried to show Burt the bathroom. Fifteen minutes later, Lancaster was chatting and laughing as if nothing had happened.

A good bridge player, Burt quickly lost most of his partners when he abused them at the table. He was a founder of the Savoy Bridge Club but had to give up going there when he fought with a prominent woman member and called her an unprintable name. She threw the cards in his face. Lancaster switched to playing at home – with two tables: when he got into a fight at one, he changed to another.

Aware of his temper. Lancaster excused it somewhat by citing his 'black Irish' background, and saying that he needed to be tough to survive in the Hollywood jungle. 'People outside Hollywood don't understand how it is here,' he said. 'It's a battle to maintain a basic integrity against bull and baloney; you have to fight all the time.'

Directors John Frankenheimer (and later Michael Winner) said they wondered when and how he would explode on the set, what would set him off and release his 'potential' violence. His violence appeared to be strictly verbal, however, although the threat of physical action doubtless made his smaller would-be opponents back off. Roland Kibbee, Hecht-Hill-Lancaster's favourite in-house screenwriter, observed, 'It seems contradictory, but he actually detests violence, and I have never heard of him hitting anyone. He has always been forceful, sure-footed and strong in his opinions – although a certain mellowness has come with the years – but he is difficult only in regard to the standards he sets in his work. He is thoroughly honest, his candour can be brutal, but he is critically and constructively valuable at production conferences. He is, to put it as simply as possible, an unusual man. He fits no moulds.'

Lancaster also insisted that his anger was totally controlled on screen. 'Energy is apparently something I've always had plenty of,' he said, 'or good health, which is the same thing. Acting is a trade; when we act we let off neurotic steam, but it is not just a wild form of expression. When I act, I am just as controlled as a man who makes watch springs.'

His 'neurotic steam' was about to be directed at star character parts: Roberta Ashley, then a writer for *This Week*, later an editor at *Cosmopolitan*, suggested at this time, in the early 1960's, that Lancaster was acting with his hair. Ashley noted that in conventional vehicles his hair seemed to be scruffily his own, but every time he was doing an unconventional part in a 'serious' movie, he did something rather dramatic to his hair in terms of colour or cut. That tendency was to become even more pronounced with *Birdman of Alcatraz*.

Hill agreed that Lancaster was making the transition to seriousness. 'At thirty-three he was a thing of beauty,' Hill recalled, 'but now he's had to make this transformation into an actor. How many of them have? He's a rarity.'

Birdman of Alcatraz, released in 1962, was the story of then seventy-three-year-old Robert Stroud, a murderer of two people who first had been sentenced to solitary confinement in 1909, and was to stay there for the rest of his life. Initially obstreperous as a prisoner (his second killing was a guard, in jail), Stroud began to study and raise birds in his cell, becoming an expert on their diseases and writing several books. The project, based on a bestselling biography by Thomas E. Gaddis, was a particular priority of Lancaster's both as producer and performer. The federal Bureau of Prisons refused to cooperate, and the island prison of Alcatraz itself was off-limits for location filming. But Gaddis's book had sold a total of five million copies, and Lancaster had a 'strong, almost maniacal concern with the whole problem of penology', he said. 'I did an enormous amount of reading. I talked to judges, I read every letter that Stroud wrote.'

Hecht-Hill-Lancaster hired English director Charles Crichton to guide the project, but after three weeks of fighting with Burt over the concept of *Birdman of Alcatraz*, and Hecht's dissatisfaction with the filming, Crichton was fired. Lancaster summoned Frankenheimer, who reluctantly agreed to direct if drastic revisions were made on the screenplay – and on the condition that only he, not the star, would direct the movie.

Frankenheimer had wanted to do the same story on television several years before, but had been put off by the networks, which were being pressured by the Bureau of Prisons. *Birdman of Alcatraz* turned out to be a long film (147 minutes), but a convincing depiction of the loneliness and despair of prison life. Whether or not it is the real Stroud story remains open to question. The Bureau of Prisons claimed Stroud was far more dangerous than he was seen to be in *Birdman of Alcatraz*, which also ignores the subject of his homosexuality. Nor does the movie answer the question of

[125]

why, after he became a model citizen, his twenty-four parole requests over the years were consistently denied.

Lancaster felt that none of this mattered very much. 'I believed principally that it was a very good story. The fact that it dealt with inadequacies in our penal system was important and worthy of being exploited, but the most compelling thing to me was the emotional story of this man and what he had gone through. We hoped to make people aware of the inadequacies of the treatment of prisoners in general and the room for improvement in the handling of criminals. But I also wanted to tell a story that would touch people emotionally. I never met this man Robert Stroud, but I felt I knew him intimately. I've never been so involved in a part before or since. When I would play scenes I would actually start to weep before they turned the camera. I couldn't control myself, I was so deeply involved. I remember John Frankenheimer used to say "Oh that's marvellous". And I would say, "No John, let the audience cry, not me." '

Birdman of Alcatraz began with Stroud, in his early thirties, already in jail, denied the right to see his visiting mother (Thelma Ritter), which results in his killing the prison guard. Through the efforts of his mother, who takes the case all the way to President Woodrow Wilson's White House, Stroud's death sentence is commuted to solitary confinement. The story, as narrated by the author Gaddis (played by Edmond O'Brien), then shows Stroud slowly developing his interest in birds after finding a lame sparrow in the prison exercise yard. After writing his first book on bird diseases he is visited by a widow (Betty Field), who proposes to market the bird medicines he has developed in his cell. He later marries the woman, which leads to a permanent estrangement from his mother. Gaddis meets his subject only once, when Stroud is transferred from Alcatraz in 1959, and the author waits for him on a San Francisco wharf. This confrontation scene is one of the most moving in the picture.

'Authorities will quarrel that Stroud was not exactly the kind of man we portrayed him to be,' Lancaster acknowledged. 'In a certain sense that might be true. But in a very real sense it isn't true. It is not a question of whether Stroud was a good man or a bad man. Society simply hasn't found out yet how criminals ought to be treated. They are still part of the old school of punishment. I don't mean to imply that the answers are easy; it's very difficult to know what is the best system. But society tends to want to shut them away and put out of sight those who have offended society. Those who are left with the task of being the keepers are not sure how to treat them. They work under deplorable conditions themselves. There have been great steps taken in recent years, now that we understand the psychology of man more than we did. But it is still at best a faulty operation, and so in that respect *Birdman of Alcatraz* is unquestionably true and no reasonable man can deny it.'

Lancaster, who aged beautifully in *Birdman of Alcatraz*, played Stroud with obvious compassion. *Time* said the actor portrayed the prisoner 'with a firm restraint that never conceals a deep-felt conviction that Stroud should not be in stir at all.' *The New York Times* agreed that Lancaster's acting was 'notable for realism, nuance and restraint'. For his work in *Birdman of Alcatraz*, Burt received his third Academy Award nomination, his third New York Film Critics Award and the Best Actor Award at the Venice Film Festival. Harold Hecht was seemingly the only one who was not entirely pleased with *Birdman of Alcatraz*. 'Burt became obsessed by Stroud,' Hecht said. 'People are compelled to become what they are by the special circumstances of their lives. Look at Stroud and look at Burt. Burt became an actor because he's locked in too.'

'The film wasn't a great success,' Lancaster acknowledged years later, 'but now people constantly talk to me about it. It proves something, but I don't know what. If I could prepare myself as thoroughly for every part as I did for *Birdman of Alcatraz* I'd be happy. The movie was important to me, because it stated that a man's potential can never be judged by the evil he does. There is always something good somewhere.'

During the filming of *Birdman of Alcatraz*, Burt's brother Jim, who had been working as an assistant director, dropped dead of a heart attack on the set, one day after lunch. The body was removed, and Lancaster continued working, although the company expected him to quit. Whatever grief he felt at Jim's death was private, and deferred.

Birdman of Alcatraz was the last movie produced by Hecht-Hill-Lancaster, which dissolved after its release. Although Lancaster's recent pictures had been admirable in many ways, they were not the hoped-for financial successes that any production company needs to carry on, and Hecht-Hill-Lancaster had begun to lose money. 'We had taken on some of the overheadaches of a major studio,' Burt recalled, 'and could no longer afford to operate the way we wanted to. You can't spend two or three years preparing for a film that will have limited appeal, when your overhead is the size of ours.' While Hecht felt that the company could have survived if Lancaster had 'hung in there', the star reasoned, 'When a marriage is over, it's over, and there's no use staying together for the sake of the children.'

In 1962 Burt was persuaded, against his better judgment, to make an appearance on Mike Wallace's television talk show, *PM*. Whenever he did break his no-publicity rule it was to promote a project he believed in, in this case *Birdman of Alcatraz*. But Burt had made it clear to Wallace – whose reputation as a tough, even nasty, interviewer was already established – that he would only talk about his work within the framework of an agreed-upon list of questions. Wallace almost immediately began badgering Lancaster about his temper vis-à-vis his co-stars, particularly the arguments on *Judgment at Nuremberg*.

'There no reason to talk about it,' said Lancaster, glaring angrily at the host. 'My temper belongs to me.'

Wallace said he was trying to be thorough and honest. Lancaster, even more furious, shouted, 'I am suggesting you are not. I think this line of questioning is unreasonable.'

The host then claimed that since Lancaster was the guest on the show he had no choice but to answer Wallace's questions. Burt disagreed: 'You won't have the advantage long if we keep going on like this.' Then he got up from his seat and walked out of the television studio.

Social consciousness brought Stanley Kramer and Lancaster together in 1963 for *A Child Is Waiting*, which dealt with the problems of teaching retarded children. Kramer produced, Abby Mann wrote the script from his own *Studio One* television play, and actor John Cassavetes directed. The picture was filmed on location at the Pacific State Hospital in Pomona, California, whose inmates played all but the most important of the juvenile roles. Lancaster played the superintendent of

[129]

the institution, while Judy Garland, his co-star from *Judgment at Nuremberg*, played a new staff member who disagrees with Lancaster's stern approach, and becomes particularly attached to one problem child.

Arthur Knight wrote, in *Saturday Review*, 'Garland and Lancaster radiate a warmth so genuine that one is certain that the children are responding to them, not merely following some vaguely comprehended script,' but he found Cassavetes' direction 'awkward'.

John Huston and Lancaster were also reunited in 1963, thanks to Kirk Douglas, who invited Burt, Frank Sinatra, Robert Mitchum and Tony Curtis to be disguised guest stars in his English murder mystery movie, *The List of Adrian Messenger*, directed by Huston. The four guest stars, heavily disguised and made up, were offered up as possible murderers and the movie audience was invited to guess who was whom. At the end of the film, the four unmasked for those who hadn't guessed, and the large suffragette turned out to be Lancaster. While many critics found *The List of Adrian Messenger* too gimmicky for its own good, Judith Crist in the New York *Herald-Tribune* called the movie 'absorbing and intelligent'.

CHAPTER TEN

The Leopard

LANCASTER HAD LONG been an admirer of foreign films, and with his new freedom from the confines of Hecht-Hill-Lancaster, he was now free to make them. 'When I was a kid,' he said, 'I was aware that fine films were coming from abroad. Some of the early French and English films had a great deal to say. They were not necessarily popular in the United States. You'd see them in New York in small theatres; it's ironic that a film like *La Grande Illusion* should only play at a small theatre, but it did. The feeling of exhibitors was that people wouldn't be interested. But that's all changed. The world of film is international now.'

In 1962, Goffredo Lombardo, the Italian producer who was preparing the movie version of *The Leopard* to be directed by Luchino Visconti, visited Hollywood in an attempt to sign Lancaster for 'an adventure story, a *Ben-Hur* type of movie. But it was a poor script, and I wasn't interested,' Lancaster recalled. 'Then he noticed that I had a copy of [Giuseppe] Lampedusa's novel *The Leopard* on my desk. "Would you like to play the role?"

he said. I said, "Oh, I can't play the role. It calls for a real Italian." When Lombardo went home, he suggested to Visconti the possibility of using me. Visconti said: "Aghh, terrible – he's a cowboy, a gangster actor – awful, awful, no, no, no." Then he saw *Judgment at Nuremberg*, in which I played a dignified, kind of aristocratic character, and was impressed by it. He was also impressed by how much I knew about the background of the Leopard character.

'Actually he was having trouble finding an Italian actor to fit the physical requirements that he wanted. The book describes the Prince as being a tall, blond, blue-eyed man of German heritage as well as Italian. At first Visconti wanted the great Russian actor, Nikolai Cherkassov, who had worked with Eisenstein and done *Don Quixote* and *Ivan the Terrible*. Visconti went to Russia to see Cherkassov and discovered that the man was too old, almost seventy. Then he decided to use Olivier, a classical actor for a classic role. Olivier was engaged to do it, but before he signed the contract, he was asked to head the new National Theatre, which was something he was very anxious to do, and the shooting schedule for *The Leopard* was over five months.'

Visconti, who had written the screenplay with four collaborators, needed three million dollars from Twentieth Century-Fox to finance *The Leopard*. The studio agreed on the condition that a major international star be cast as the Prince. That situation did not leave Visconti with much leverage and the Harlem street kid gangster-cowboy was signed to play the 1860s Sicilian aristocrat.

'When I arrived in Rome for *The Leopard*, I had a meeting for three hours with Visconti,' Lancaster recalled. 'He was quite surprised to find that I knew the book backwards, every nuance of it, and quite delighted to know that the people I'd lived with in my section of New York were Sicilians, and that I knew a great deal about the background of these people, and the Mafia. "Now," Visconti said to me, "I think maybe we can make the film." Visconti is really a painter, he has the eye of an artist. He thinks that way, he shoots as a director in a way that I have never seen. He will make the camera accommodate itself to what we are, to give a sense of real perspective, not a false one. It puts an enormous demand on the technicians, but he gets marvellous results – a visual artist in the best sense of the word.

'I worked with Visconti on the screenplay too. He imparted this tremendous confidence and you couldn't help but share it with him. But everything had to be exactly as he wanted in other departments. He wouldn't work unless it was so. He was a count. The Viscontis used to own Milan. He knew the leopards, those aristocrats, like the back of his hand. There was one scene where I had to open a drawer to take out some money, and when I opened it, I found magnificent silk shirts that had been made for me. I said to the cameraman, "Does the camera see these?" He said "No." I said to Visconti, "Why are they there?" He said: "You're the Prince. Is for you to touch." '

Yet, Lancaster found, 'as far as my acting was concerned, Visconti gave me complete freedom regarding the way I wanted to move, the whole acting aspect of it. There was only one time on the set when we had a long talk about the approach to one scene, and the ideas he wanted me to get across were brilliant. They were far superior to anything I had in mind. But in the main, if he thinks you're a good and thorough professional and you know what you're doing, then

[133]

he'll let you go straight ahead and do whatever you want to do. After that, he'll refine the things you've done. I was very happy with *The Leopard*. I think it was some of my best work.'

The Leopard tells the story of Prince Don Fabrizio (Lancaster), a Sicilian aristocrat at the time of the unification of Italy by Garibaldi's red shirt invasion, the 1860s. Fabrizio is threatened not only by revolution but also by the simultaneous rise of the merchant middle-class. He compromises by arranging the marriage of his nephew (Alain Delon) to the daughter (Claudia Cardinale) of his boorish but wealthy estate manager. At the slowly unfolding film's end, Fabrizio has succeeded in preserving his family's old values against the wave of the future.

'Visconti was showing the ludicrousness of this kingdom,' Lancaster said, 'these people who didn't know how to run a country, who had lost touch with reality, and yet in their peculiar way, were beyond all that. The Prince says that Garibaldi is coming to teach them manners, and then he says, "He won't succeed, because we are gods." It was true, the old prince knew the new people coming in were greedy, that nothing changes, that the new classes that attain power are as bad as the ones that lose it.'

A lushly photographed epic (at the time, 1963, it was often referred to as the Italian *Gone With The Wind*), *The Leopard* featured Visconti's typical attention to rich, minute detail. The unforgettable ballroom sequence, in which Lancaster dances with Cardinale to composer Nino Rota's 'lost' Verdi waltz, summed up the charm and manners of a Sicilian aristocracy that suddenly was to be no more. The original film ran for 205 minutes, in Italian, and was hailed a masterpiece throughout Europe, where it also did respectable business. In Great

Britain and the United States, *The Leopard* was cut by forty minutes, and dubbed into English under the supervision of Sidney Pollack and Lancaster himself. English-speaking audiences stayed away in droves, and most critics in England and America denounced *The Leopard* as a giant bore. *Time,* however, saw the film for what it is: 'a composite portrait of a time, a place and a man that finally emerges as a splendid piece of cinema. Lancaster, within definite limits, is superb.' *Variety* also saw *The Leopard* as 'an outstanding achievement', and said, 'Lancaster gives the picture some of its deeply moving moments as he moves, a sad, lónely and ageing figure in a world no longer his own.'

Although an avid filmgoer, Lancaster made a point of not seeing his own films. He made an exception for *The Leopard*, even going to a theatre to assess the audience reaction. 'There was this man behind me,' he remembered, 'who kept asking his wife, "When's Lancaster going to screw Cardinale?" And that's all he wanted to know. But I made a hell of a lot of money out of that film.'

Claudia Cardinale recalled the experience of working with Lancaster on *The Leopard* at her villa in Rome in 1983. 'We shared a love for Visconti,' she said, 'and I liked him as a very professional man and as a human being. He's very nice. He was marvellous in *The Leopard*. To become the Prince of Lampedusa like he did was really good work. Visconti was a marvellous director, but Burt did really marvellous work. It's one of his best films.'

The Leopard was re-released in America and England in 1983, in the original Italian (Lancaster's voice is dubbed), and with some of its cuts restored, for a total length of 185 minutes. A critical and popular success at the Los Angeles Film Festival, *The Leopard* went on

[135]

to get the critical upgrading it deserved, in New York and London, finally, twenty years later, vindicating Lancaster's (and Cardinale's) belief that the Visconti epic was their collective masterpiece.

Visconti, who died in 1976, said of working with Lancaster on *The Leopard:* 'The Prince himself was a very complex character – at times autocratic, rude, strong – at times romantic, good, understanding – and sometimes even stupid, and, above all, mysterious. Burt is all these things too. I sometimes think Burt is the most perfectly mysterious man I ever met in my life.'

Lancaster returned to more typical fare for him in 1964, with John Frankenheimer's *Seven Days in May.* As General James Scott, Chairman of the US Joint Chiefs of Staff, Lancaster was exposed by his aide (Kirk Douglas) as the mastermind of a planned right-wing military coup. Having become appalled by what he terms as the appeasement of the Soviet Union by pacifistic US President Fredric March, Lancaster as Scott sets up a secret base in the desert, staffing it with military men of his own persuasion. Rod Serling wrote this taut, intelligent political supposition from Fletcher Knebel's bestselling novel; both movie and book also worked as thrillers. *Seven Days in May*, in addition to pairing Lancaster and Douglas again, reunited Burt with Ava Gardner for the first time since *The Killers*, eighteen years before. Gardner this time played Lancaster's blowsy cast–off mistress, whom Douglas uses to obtain some incriminating letters from the general.

Douglas, although the producer of the movie, was notably jealous of Lancaster throughout the filming of *Seven Days in May*, according to director Frankenheimer, who said: 'Kirk wanted to be Burt Lancaster – he's wanted to be Burt Lancaster all his life.'

'It was at this time that our friendship was really put

[136]

to the test,' Lancaster recalled, 'because I found myself being directed by him in every scene I played with Kirk. I really didn't mind, because by then I had developed a profound respect for Kirk because of his production of the film *Spartacus*. Not because of his production of the film, which was superb, not because of his work as an actor in the film, which was superb, but because single-handedly he ended the disgraceful Hollywood Blacklist, by using Dalton Trumbo's name openly as the writer of *Spartacus*. Until then, members of the blacklist were writing covertly, under the table, so to speak. Or they weren't working at all, which was usually the case.'

Much of *Seven Days in May* was filmed in Washington, DC, with full government cooperation. President John F. Kennedy, although he did not live to see the final film, said he felt it was a movie that should be made. Lancaster, playing against his own pro-Kennedy convictions, was especially effective among a first-rate cast. Instead of playing the general as a strident villain, he made the man seem rational, calmly calculating and quiet. On release in 1964, *Seven Days in May* was both a box office and a critical success. Judith Crist, in the New York *Herald-Tribune*, said 'Burt Lancaster combines a finely controlled fanaticism with innate conviction.'

Lancaster fought with director Arthur Penn on his next project, *The Train*, and after two weeks of filming in Paris, Penn was replaced because of creative differences with Lancaster and producer Jules Bricken. Burt then telephoned John Frankenheimer in Hollywood to ask him to take over. Frankenheimer was exhausted from *Seven Days in May* and at first refused. He finally agreed to do it as a personal favour to Lancaster, and read the script for the first time while flying across the Atlantic to France, making notes for drastic changes.

[137]

In the meantime, Associate Producer Bernard Farrell acted as director on *The Train*.

The Train was an American-Italian-French co-production, released by United Artists in 1965. Based on a novel by Rose Alland, the movie, Lancaster's last in black and white, had the feel of a documentary with a strong sense of its place and period, France in 1944. The story is about a German colonel, played by Paul Scofield, who wants to ship a trainload of valuable paintings from Paris to Germany, in the face of the allied advance. Lancaster, as a French railway inspector who has no interest in art but is a member of the Resistance, is determined not to lose the paintings for France. He deceives the Germans on board the train into thinking it has passed into German territory, when all it has done is make a circle within France back to its original starting point. The colonel then takes French hostages on the front of the train and heads towards Germany. The tale is climaxed by a train wreck, accomplished by special effects man Lee Zavitz, who had staged the burning of Atlanta in *Gone With the Wind*. At the end, the German soldiers have deserted, the French hostages are dead and only Lancaster and Scofield face each other alongside the train tracks, where the paintings lie scattered and unclaimed.

Apart from Lancaster and Scofield, the entire cast of *The Train* was French and German. The French Railway System cooperated fully in providing yards and stations as shooting locales, and even discarded rolling stock to smash up. No train models were used for the crash scenes, during which several cameras were destroyed. Lancaster did not employ a French accent in his characterisation, but he did adopt the French worker's habit of having a burning cigarette always dangling from his mouth, not a difficult gambit for a heavy smoker. Then fifty–one, Lancaster not only looked but acted a great deal younger. 'He was in his element,' said Frankenheimer, 'falling from trains, sliding down ladders, climbing walls, yet all the time living his part.'

Jeanne Moreau, playing an innkeeper who helps Lancaster's inspector hide out, was less enthusiastic about him: 'Burt Lancaster! Before he can pick up an ashtray, he discusses his motivation for an hour or two. You want to say, "Just pick up the ashtray and shut up!" '

Frankenheimer admitted, 'If Burt and I had that film to do over again, we would both do it differently. Once Burt became involved he began to live the film so intently that he said to me, "My God, if only we had started this together, I would have played it with a French accent. Then we wouldn't have had to dub the other actors into the hoarse American-English and the entire film would have been more convincing." '

Yet, Bosley Crowther, in *The New York Times*, praised Lancaster's stunting agility and found *The Train* 'intensely engrossing'. But *Time* said, 'Not for a moment does he seem to be a French patriot.'

During the filming of *The Train* in Europe, Lancaster flew to Washington for one day to join, along with Marlon Brando and other actors, Martin Luther King's March on Washington.

The Hallelujah Trail was a would-be farce-Western, filmed in Cinerama and other excesses by director John Sturges of *Gunfight at the OK Corral*. Lancaster was cast as a cavalry colonel in the winter of 1867, when Denver faces a shortage of liquor. Lee Remick leads a fanatic band of female temperance supporters who would like to keep it that way. Forty wagons, carrying 600 barrels of whiskey are sent in, to be protected from Sioux Indian attacks by a Denver militia force. The intended

[139]

spoof of pioneer epics ran almost three hours and was climaxed by a free-for-all shoot-out involving the cavalry, Indians, temperance ladies and local miners – in which no one is killed. *The Hallelujah Trail* is the closest Lancaster came to playing comedy in movies until *Local Hero* in 1983. In *Hallelujah*, however, Burt is more of the straight man who allows the broad comedy to surround him. But his biggest laugh comes when Remick, interrupted in her harangue on the evils of drink, beards Burt in his bathroom, where he is relaxing in his tub, reading his newspaper and smoking a cigar. As Remick resumes her sermon, Lancaster looks up and takes the cigar slowly from his mouth to say, 'You'll excuse me if I don't stand up?'

While *The Hallelujah Trail* was neither a hit with the public nor reviewers, Lancaster's next movie, *The Professionals* was both. Richard Brooks and Burt reunited for this out-and-out adventure story of four soldiers of fortune hired by millionaire Ralph Bellamy to retrieve his abducted wife (Claudia Cardinale) from Mexico. Brooks wrote the screenplay from a novel by Frank O'Rourke, *A Mule for the Marquesa*, as well as directing. Burt naturally assumed that he would play the leading role of the leader of the mercenaries, which went in fact to Lee Marvin, who was under contract to the producing studio, Columbia, and coming off his Oscar-winning performance in *Cat Ballou*. Brooks set Lancaster straight, telling him he couldn't be the boss: 'That won't work, that's no good at all.'

'How d'you figure that out, Richard?' Lancaster asked, losing his smile.

'Because, Burt, when you give orders with your stiff upper lip and all that, you're boring. This guy you'll play is a dynamiter, a clown, he's funny.'

'Dynamiter? There's no dynamiter in the book.'

'There will be by the time we get to do the movie.'

'What will my character be like?' asked Lancaster.

'Like you, Burt, he's funny, and good at his job, and a hell of a pro.'

'Okay, as long as we start by October.'

Lancaster threw himself into the part of an explosives expert who takes the commission to get away from the husbands of his most recent conquests. Marvin, as an ex-Army munitions specialist, liked bossing everyone around, especially a star of Lancaster's stature. Robert Ryan played a horse breeder, and Woody Strode completed the foursome as a black bow-and-arrow and knife expert. These professionals take on the dangerous mission of rescuing Cardinale from the camp of one of Pancho Villa's strongest *compadres* (Jack Palance) in revolution-rent Mexico. They accomplish their purpose with a great deal of violence and cunning, only to discover that Cardinale and Palance are really lovers and she refuses to return. The American band takes her along anyway, with Palance and his men in fierce pursuit. *The Professionals* was filmed in Nevada's Valley of Fire State Park, with the fifty-three-year-old Lancaster in full athletic flower, a charming scoundrel fighting over a woman again.

During the filming of *The Professionals*, Lancaster broke his rule against entertaining co-stars by having Claudia Cardinale to his house, which she appreciated. 'I was a bit lost in Hollywood,' she recalled, 'it was my first time there, and he was very sweet to invite me to his home to see his family.'

Saturday Review's Arthur Knight said of the movie, 'A rock-solid professionalism pervades every shot, every line and every performance.' Judith Crist, in the New York *World-Journal-Tribune*, wrote that, 'Lancaster has never been more athletically suave.'

[141]

The Scalphunters was also a comedy-Western, set on the pre-Civil War American frontier, but this time filmed in Mexico. Although essentially an entertainment, *The Scalphunters* also had a serious pro-civil rights stand to take. Lancaster played a fur trapper passing through Kiowa Indian country; he is ambushed by the Indians, who steal his pelts and leave him with an escaped slave (Ossie Davis) whom the Kiowas captured from the Comanches. Trapper and slave team up to track the Indians and retrieve the furs, but a band of scalphunters led by Telly Savalas and his cigar-smoking mistress (Shelley Winters) have killed the Indians and taken the furs. Lancaster and Davis join the scalphunters, only to have another tribe of Indians run off with Winters as a new squaw for their chief – and the pelts. The racial relationships are treated with humour, and after a long period of getting on each other's nerves, Lancaster and Davis battle it out in a mudpuddle, both coming up a medium brown, which makes them equal after all.

During the filming of *The Scalphunters*, in 1967, Lancaster and Pollack fought frequently on the set, but at night Burt studied Spanish with a tutor, and attended a Gian-Carlo Menotti festival at the opera house in Durango.

Vincent Canby, in *The New York Times*, said that Lancaster gave *The Scalphunters* 'its unifying vitality'. Other critics liked the picture as well and it was a modest hit for United Artists in 1968.

With Shelley Winters, *The Scalphunters*, 1968

As Neddy Merrill in *The Swimmer*, 1968

With Deborah Kerr, *The Gypsy Moths*, 1969

Valdez is Coming, 1971

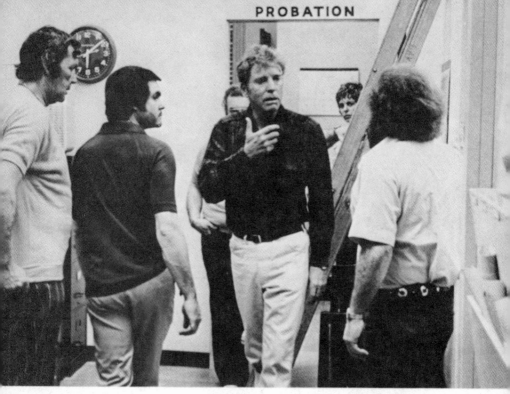

Directing *The Midnight Man*, 1974

With Robert Ryan, *Executive Action*, 1974

As Moses, 1975

As Dr Moreau, 1977

With Rod Steiger, *Cattle Annie and Little Britches*, 1981

With Susan Sarandon, *Atlantic City*, 1981

As Felix Happer in *Local Hero*, 1983

The Osterman Weekend, 1983

CHAPTER ELEVEN

The Swimmer

ALTHOUGH HE OWNED a $30,000 swimming pool, with a waterfall, heating system and a tributary into his Bel-Air living room (just about the fanciest and most expensive model available in 1966), Lancaster still had mild hydrophobia and had not really enjoyed swimming since those quarter-mile sprints to Ward's Island off East Harlem. But if Burt was embarrassed about having to take three months worth of swimming lessons to overcome his fear, he never let on. Certainly his hydrophobia didn't show on film, which was a good thing since *The Swimmer* is about a man who makes a nine-pool, eight-mile, cross county swim and portage to his home. Burt as the man, Neddy Merrill, played the entire picture in his bathing suit, or less. The screenplay by Eleanor Perry (then married to the director) was adapted from a short story by John Cheever, who had set it in the toniest suburbs of New York City. For that reason – and because Hollywood pools, especially Lancaster's, were deemed far too posh – *The Swimmer* was filmed in Connecticut's Fairfield County.

Director Frank Perry and *The Swimmer*'s producers picked the most private locations for Lancaster's marathon swim, paying local home owners about $500 apiece for the privilege of splashing about in their pools for a few days. An important stipulation was that the cast and crew would use portable toilet facilities and eat from catering wagons, not go traipsing into residents' houses. Lancaster took a star's prerogative to make himself the sole exception to that rule. One evening he appeared in a terrycloth robe at one back door and asked: 'Are you the lady of the house? I'm Burt Lancaster. May I have a vodka martini?' He was given the drink. A Fairfield County buzz-saw operator whose pursuit of his livelihood was messing up *The Swimmer* soundtrack was paid $200 to stop sawing for the day, prompting other locals to pull out their power lawnmowers and other noisy appliances in hopes of more hush money.

Although *The Swimmer* is Neddy Merrill's story, he is accompanied on his unusual Sunday afternoon sojourn at least part of the way by Janet Landgard, playing his children's former babysitter all grown up. Usually they have the pools all to themselves, even when groups of drinkers are congregating around them, but on one of their splashes they encounter a man who is drifting around the pool in an inner tube, with a party hat on his head and martini glass in his hand. He is obviously stoned. Lancaster and Landgard attempt to shake the man into consciousness, without success. They swim the length of the pool and move on to the next one. Author John Cheever was offered the role of the floating souse, but declined. 'If I'm only going to be in one movie in my life,' he said, 'I'm damned if my grandchildren are going to see me drunk in a swimming pool.' Instead, Cheever took a less significant role as a pool party guest. 'All I did,' he recalled, 'was say "Hi", shake Lancaster's hand and kiss Janet Landgard, which I liked.' Members of the Lake Club of New Canaan, Connecticut, were paid five dollars a day to work as extras in the party sequence.

The Swimmer's swim is a metaphor for his failed life, which is revealed in conversations along the way. At first he seems good-naturedly sane, if eccentric, but gradually he is seen to be out of his mind. The movie climaxes with a visit to his former mistress, and ends with him arriving at his own front door; the house has long been deserted. Lancaster at age fifty-three when the film was made in 1966, presented the lithe frame of a man of fifteen years younger, and he was still something of a box office draw. But the special, even eerie quality and content of *The Swimmer*, abetted by Marvin Hamlisch's haunting score, made it a difficult picture for executive producer Sam Spiegel and Columbia to distribute. Spiegel, in particular, objected to the scene between Merrill and his former mistress and insisted that it be re-shot with a different actress. Frank and Eleanor Perry protested, then withdrew. At Lancaster's suggestion, Columbia then hired Sidney Pollack to direct the new mistress sequence, with Janice Rule replacing Barbara Loden in the part. Since it does have a different director, and was shot in California rather than Connecticut, the scene is jarringly alien to the rest of *The Swimmer*.

Although *The Swimmer* was dumped on the market unceremoniously, finally, in 1968, it never had a chance to find even a cult audience until years later. Vincent Canby in *The New York Times* termed it 'a grim, disturbing, and sometimes funny view of a very special segment of upper-middle-class American life'. Judith Crist, in *New York* magazine called Lancaster's acting 'pehaps the best of his career', and the film itself 'a triumph'.

Despite their differences on *The Scalphunters*, Lancaster and Sidney Pollack were able to get together again a year later for *Castle Keep*. Filmed entirely on location in Yugoslavia, *Castle Keep* was an adaptation of William Eastlake's bestselling novel about a one-eyed major (Lancaster), who leads his men to occupy an important tenth-century castle in Belgium's Ardennes Forest. The castle belongs to an elderly, impotent count (Jean-Pierre Aumont), who arranges for the major to father a child by his young countess, in order to give him an heir. Instead of joining the ordered Allied retreat, Lancaster's major decides to stay to defend the castle against the German attack. In the final battle, everything and everyone is destroyed except the young wife (Astrid Hereen) and a black private (Al Freeman, Jnr), who narrates the story.

The expensive Filmways-Columbia production, which involved a huge cast, battalions of extras, and the construction of the castle itself, attempted to be an intelligent person's anti-war satire. But its pretentious dialogue and portentious symbolism combine with oddly inserted low comedy and dead-on combat scenes, causing *Castle Keep* to fall leadenly between the two stools of serious commentary and silly send-up. Lancaster's character seems to be perfectly sane and rational, yet chooses the certain death of trying to protect his fortress from the overwhelming German army. Vincent Canby in *The New York Times* wrote that *Castle Keep* was 'never as impressive as the sum of its very expensive parts'. William Wolf in *Cue* called it 'the most unusual of war movies', but added that 'the artistry to bring it off successfully simply isn't there.'

Pollack and Lancaster, although they should have

known better from *The Scalphunters*, fought so badly at the beginning of production on *Castle Keep* that the young leading lady packed her bags and quit the production. She had already arrived at the airport before star and director discovered her absence and convinced her to return. Burt's ladyfriend, Jackie Bone, a former hairdresser, then thirty-seven or so, had first appeared publicly during the filming of *The Swimmer*. Now, on *Castle Keep* in Yugoslavia, she and Lancaster had some heated fights. Not having Burt's physical restraint, Jackie heaved a bottle at his head, which landed him in the hospital.

Deborah Kerr and Lancaster were reunited sixteen years after *From Here to Eternity* in *The Gypsy Moths*. John Frankenheimer directed Burt, for the fifth and last time, in this adventure story (by William Hanley, from the novel by James Drought) about three sky divers who barnstorm a small Kansas town. The trio of divers (Lancaster, Gene Hackman and Scott Wilson) arrives in town to stay at the home of Wilson's aunt (Kerr). She is unhappily married to a professor (William Windom), who is indifferent even when she and Lancaster have an affair. She refuses to uproot herself to leave with Lancaster, who fails to pull the parachute release during a dangerous jump the next day, and falls to his death.

The Gypsy Moths was filmed on location in Kansas, and its aerial stunts (filmed from simultaneously falling parachutes by Carl Boenisch) were its best feature. The subtext of human self-destructiveness (drawn like moths to the flame) is far less successful, and the Kerr-Lancaster reunion made for better advance publicity than it did any on-screen magic. *Life* noted that 'One is uncomfortably reminded of the romance these two enacted in *From Here to Eternity* – and of the passage of

[147]

time since,' although Lancaster was praised: 'As he has grown older, Mr Lancaster has developed a capacity, unique in established stars, to "give away" scenes that his status in the movie pecking order entitles him to dominate. He did it in *Castle Keep*, he does it in *The Gypsy Moths* and he deserves full credit for his shrewd selflessness.'

No one had higher praise for Lancaster, however, than director Frankenheimer. After five pictures and countless fights, he could say, 'He is one of the most hard-working individuals I have ever met. He cares deeply about what he does. He's very considerate of other actors. I think he's one of the few actors I've met who knows something about production; he knows something about cutting, about the problems of making a film. I find it easy to work with him. When he's been correctly cast, there is nobody better.'

In July 1969, Lancaster's twenty-two-year marriage to Norma Anderson ended. As a result of the divorce – on the grounds of mental cruelty – that she was granted in the Santa Monica court famous for movie star divorces, Norma was given custody of the three minor children, daughters Susan, Joanna and Sighle, and half of more than two million dollars. Neither Norma nor Lancaster made any public statement about the end of the marriage.

By 1970, Lancaster was no longer big box office and his salaries and participation deals were getting smaller. He seemingly did not care, as he did a long series of introspective or experimental films in the late 1960's, unbroken as in the old days by a surefire Western or adventure story. *The Professionals* had been Burt's last big hit, and that was an ensemble success. *Airport*, an all-star movie version of Arthur Hailey's novel produced by Ross Hunter and directed by George

[148]

Seaton, brought back box office success. In the pivotal role of the airport manager, Lancaster had responsibility over a record blizzard, an attempted bombing of the plane in flight (by Van Heflin), and a stowaway (Helen Hayes) – not to mention distractions from his brother-in-law (Dean Martin) and his mistress (Jacqueline Bissett), his own unhappy marriage (to Dana Wynter), that of his sister (Barbara Hale) and his own mistress (Jean Seberg). George Kennedy as the airport's troubleshooter and Maureen Stapleton as the bomber's wife were also in the large cast. Lancaster later called the six million dollar Universal movie 'a piece of junk', but the public flocked to this *Grand Hotel* of the air, spawning three (unsuccessful) sequels and two (successful) spoofs, *Airplane* I and II.

Hayes, who won an Oscar for her supporting role as the stowaway, and Stapleton, who was nominated against her, took the acting honours in *Airport*. Archer Winsten in *The New York Post* said that the movie had 'no single letdown in its two hours and seventeen minutes'. *Independent Film Journal* cited *Airport* as 'a sure-fire audience movie [of which] critical analysis is probably superfluous, for, despite the absurdities of plot and casting, the film does work.' *Airport* was a big summer G-rated movie, in what had become an 'X' and 'R' industry, and it was a tremendous hit from the day of its opening at New York's Radio City Music Hall – although, of course, it was never shown on airplanes.

Lancaster was a dedicated supporter of Martin Luther King, Jnr, and in 1970 he donated his time to appear in a two-and-a-half-hour documentary about the late civil rights leader's life, *King: a Filmed Record...Montgomery to Memphis*. Sidney Lumet and Joseph L. Mankiewicz directed several show business celebrities, including Paul Newman, Charlton Heston, Ruby Dee,

[149]

Sidney Poitier, James Earl Jones and Joanne Woodward in tribute readings that were interspersed with documentary footage. These segments were even longer in a special five-and-a-half-hour version of *King* that was distributed to college campuses. 'While their contributions are commendable,' wrote Ann Guarino in the New York *Daily News* of Lancaster and the other celebrities, 'they serve to lengthen the film unnecessarily. The recordings and newsreels of King have enough drama as it is.'

The early 1970s found Lancaster in a reflective mood, and he even briefly considered selling off his Bel-Air mansion (more 'plastic modern' in its rebuilding than before the fire), to move to a farm in the Middle West. 'You can't live by swimming pools alone,' he explained. 'Think of the starving children. It has been a constant source of guilt to me that I have become so luckily rich. But I haven't yet found a method of salving my conscience, though I give a lot away to good causes. The trouble with money, when you have it in bags, is that you don't count it. I'm interested in having any project with which I'm connected make money, but I'm not greedy for myself. I don't have to worry about money now. When I do act in a film, I ask myself, "How can we do this so effectively that people will be moved to laughter or tears or whatever?" To me that's the yardstick.'

His only regret, he said, was that no one took him seriously as a comic actor. 'I'd love to do a straight comedy,' he said, 'but nobody thinks I'm funny. I don't mean that I could be a comic, but I could do comedy.'

Lancaster turned down the title role in *Patton*, having been the first choice of Twentieth Century-Fox. (Lee Marvin and John Wayne also turned it down before it was offered to Oscar-winner and refuser, George C.

Scott.) 'Now it's ridiculous for me to assume that every picture I do has some great theme in which I sit on the right hand of God,' said Burt. 'I've tried to hit at some modern, important subjects. I hope I've left something to be remembered by. When I go out I've a feeling it will be like the old soldier: I'll just drift quietly off. Some actors go on for ever, into the grave. I don't want to be like that.'

Valdez is Coming was the first of a trio of Westerns that Lancaster undertook in 1971-72. In his late fifties and still in fine shape, he almost seemed to be looking at last for ways to play his real age or even, in the case of the other two Westerns, *Lawman* and *Ulzana's Raid*, a character older than himself. In *Valdez is Coming*, Lancaster plays an ageing Mexican-American constable in a small town near the border. He is a victim of subtle racial prejudice in that when all is quiet he has the respect of the locals, but when he gets in trouble they do not defend or assist him. Valdez is forced to kill an innocent suspected murderer in self-defence, and is then beaten by a band of the real killers (led by Jon Cypher) when he attempts to help his victim's Indian widow.

Valdez, shot in Spain and directed by Edwin Sherin, did allow Lancaster, on screen, 'a brief fling with Susan Clark, but not like in the old days where it all ends sweetly. I'm too old to get the girl any more. Filmgoers these days aren't about to accept me winning the girl in movies, although I've been doing it pretty well for more than twenty-five years. For me romance is out. Soon I'll be pushing sixty, so I can't go chasing some young woman. I can still play leading men, but guys with more character than sex appeal.'

In the spring and summer of 1971, Lancaster returned to the stage for the first time in twenty-six years, to play an older man who does get the girl: Peter Stuy-vesant, the Dutch governor of New York City in the 1600s, in Maxwell Anderson and Kurt Weill's musical *Knickerbocker Holiday*. Walter Huston had introduced the role on Broadway in 1938, stopping the show with the immortal 'September Song'. Nelson Eddy played Stuyvesant in United Artists' unfortunate 1944 film version. Lancaster called this role, in which he not only had to sing, but play the entire part, dancing and wooing, on one leg (with his real leg doubled up in a 'straitjacket'), 'the most challenging of my career'. To remind everyone that he was at least a frustrated singer, Lancaster in April made a second performing appearance on the Academy Awards telecast, singing a nominated song. *Knickerbocker Holiday* opened on 11 May 1971 in San Francisco, where it stayed for seven weeks, moving to Los Angeles for an eight-week run in July and August. Each night Burt sang 'September Song' and four other numbers.

Lancaster described his singing voice, prior to his opening in San Francisco, as 'a bass-baritone, very light in texture, and designed to move most people out of the theatre. However, I have the finest, most expensive voice teacher in the world, Frank Sinatra. Frank offered to do it purely out of friendship, when I asked him to suggest someone who could work with me. We've been going at it three or four times a week.'

'Oddly enough, his singing isn't at all bad,' Dan Sullivan reported of Lancaster's performance, in the *Los Angeles Times*. 'It's the acting side of the role that gives him trouble. To begin with, he is no more comfortable in period dress on the stage than he is on the screen. Secondly, he has to hop around on a silver peg-leg that gives him too much to think about. Finally, he is simply not at home in sly, twinkling, mock-ferocious comedy.

Lines that ought to come out with deft irony sound like heavy camp, as if the actor were doing a parody [television] guest shot. It's an uphill fight all the way, and the applause at the end is more for effort than achievement.'

During the Los Angeles run of *Knickerbocker Holiday*, Lancaster was arrested for alleged drunk driving. It was at three in the morning of 6 August 1971, in Malibu, as Burt and Jackie were returning home from a party after the performance. He was released in Jackie Bone's custody, and at a jury trial in a Los Angeles municipal court was acquitted of the charge; he testified that he had had only one beer and one martini at the party, and the jury believed him. Earlier, Burt had helped Jackie out of a similar situation in Rome. She was accused of driving in an area of the city banned to automobiles. Jackie, in turn accused the police of taking ninety dollars from her passport folder when they examined her papers. She was jailed overnight in Rome's Rebibbia facility, but extricated by Burt the next morning, when the incident was dropped.

Lawman took Lancaster back to the more familiar clothes and territory of a conventional Western. Filmed in Mexico, and both produced and directed by the Englishman Michael Winner, it features Lancaster as a marshal. He tracks the men who invaded his town and killed a man, to the small Western town of Sabbath, where the sheriff (Robert Ryan) suggests he not pursue the suspects since most of them work for the powerful local mogul (Lee J. Cobb). Lancaster's marshal ignores the advice, although he is temporarily dissuaded by an old love (Sheree North), and ends up killing Cobb's son, leading Cobb to commit suicide.

In 1972 Lancaster made one of his rare television appearances, on the Public Broadcasting Corporation's

Sesame Street, in which he recited the alphabet from A to Z. The segment was repeated often on the education series.

Lancaster's last Western was *Ulzana's Raid,* in which he did not play the title part of the savage Indian. 'I have played Indians,' he laughed, 'a long time ago.' Instead he played a grizzled old man, who is provided as a guide to fresh-faced West Point graduate Bruce Davison, whose first assignment is to find the fierce Ulzana (Joaquin Martinez). In the course of their search, Lancaster tells Davison that, 'hating the Apaches would be like hating the desert because there ain't no water in it.' The old man, McIntosh, gradually gains the neophyte officer's respect. 'What bothers you Lieutenant', he tells the younger man, 'is that you don't like to think of white men behaving like Indians; it kind of confuses the issue.' Their mission is ultimately successful, but Lancaster's character is fatally wounded, and he chooses to stay in the desert to die, while Davison returns to headquarters to turn in his report. *Ulzana's Raid* was directed by Robert Aldrich, reteaming with Lancaster for the fourth time. Besides its arty dialogue, there was enough violence in the picture to give it an 'R' rating.

Defending the violence as necessary to portray the Indian as a brutal savage, Lancaster said 'that's what he was. He was also, as we brought out, highly moral, had his own code of ethics, his own religion. We were trying to draw a parallel to a condition like Vietnam, say, where the Americans don't know the people, don't understand them, and don't even care to. This is what happened when the white man went West. Another point we make is that the white man had many of the same bloody instincts as the Indian, only they were kept in check by the thin veneer of civilisation. But

[154]

the Indians did kill savagely and brutally – they were probably driven to it by the way they were treated, by the way they were debilitated, by the fact that they were taken from their lands and confined to reservations where their spirits began to die. Ulzana tries to rekindle them. I loved doing the picture. I thought the script was very well written. The author, Alan Sharpe, is very talented, and the whole approach to the Indian problem, the whole background, I found highly interesting.'

Michael Winner and Lancaster joined forces again in 1973, for *Scorpio*, Burt's rather belated entry into the late 1960s cold-war spy genre. To bolster Burt's sagging box office appeal (none of the three Westerns had done well, but then that whole genre was in decline), two of his former co-stars were added to the cast. Alain Delon plays a young assassin hired to kill Lancaster's CIA agent, of whom the young man is a student and devotee. Paul Scofield, as an urbane and retired Russian spy living in Vienna, engages Lancaster in a brandy-induced reminiscence in *Scorpio*'s most memorable scene, in which they conclude that 'there are no more secrets, at least none worth stealing'.

Lancaster characterised *Scorpio* as 'an entertainment, a glamorous one, because of the European backgrounds. It's a CIA story, nothing incisive, just a lot of action. It's one of those things you do as part of your living, but you try to avoid doing them as much as you can. There's an awfully good cast, but it's pure entertainment, of no real lasting significance.' Despite its anachronistic emulation of mid-1960s cynical spy movies, *Variety* disagreed, '*Scorpio* might have been an acceptable action programme if its narrative were clearer, its dialogue "less cultured".'

Executive Action was also a thriller of sorts, but far

from an entertainment, since it was a speculation on the assassination of President Kennedy. Lancaster was enthusiastic in his involvement, taking a small salary in exchange for a share of the profits. The film, directed by David Miller from a Dalton Trumbo screenplay, puts forth the thesis that the killing was a right-wing plot and that Lee Harvey Oswald was set up to take the blame. Lancaster, Robert Ryan and Will Geer play the principal conspirators, with their plotting and the Oswald duping interspersed with documentary footage of the events of November 1963 in Dallas.

'I was a Kennedy man,' explained Lancaster. 'I knew there would be an outcry in some quarters, but I've never worried about what the public thinks. The only thing I took into consideration was the validity of the script. There's no question that there was a conspiracy of some sort. That's why everyone has been so dissatisfied and why so many witnesses died afterwards. The real purpose of the film – if it has any value at all – is to make people not accept things too easily.'

Lancaster made 1974's *The Midnight Man*, as co-producer, co-writer and co-director with Roland Kibbee, as a favour to Kibbee, his collaborator and friend since *Ten Tall Men*, twenty–three years before. 'It was a concession to me because I wanted to make some money,' Kibbee conceded. 'It certainly wasn't the kind of project Burt would have picked out for himself. Burt is one of the most intellectual actors I've ever known. He has no taste for pulp fiction, and his reading is on a very high level. I had to talk him into reading *The Midnight Lady and the Mourning Man*, which is pulp. He is – I'm sorry to say, since I owned pieces of some of them – absolutely cavalier about whether his pictures make money or not. Lancaster is the most uncompromising star I know of.'

The complicated whodunnit, from David Anthony's novel, is about an ex-policeman (Lancaster) who is paroled after serving a sentence for murdering his wife's lover. Working at the only job he can land, as a security man on a small South Carolina college campus, he uncovers a series of murders, which the movie has him solve in muddled fashion. Of his first credit as a director since *The Kentuckian* in 1955, Lancaster laughed, 'I've been sort of directing ever since, but this one's official. I'm cutting my ancient eye teeth on it.'

CHAPTER TWELVE

Moses

DESPITE HIS DISINCLINATION to take roles with specific religious significance, in 1975 Lancaster agreed to make his television debut in a six-part, twelve-hour mini-series entitled *Moses, the Lawgiver*. He defended his seeming inconsistency by saying that the script and the subsequent production represented 'the best thing that's been done on television, and superior to the DeMille movie [*The Ten Commandments*, starring Charlton Heston]. When I was first approached I could not see anything in it for me. I had no desire to play Moses as an historical or religious character. Then I read the Anthony Burgess script. It had a modern approach. He saw God as a very tough customer, with whom Moses was always in conflict. That appealed to me immediately: me fighting God! We show the people as very simple, rather like Bedouins. Moses comes over as a benevolent dictator. Obviously he must have been a very remarkable man.'

Moses represented Lancaster's first venture into dramatic acting specifically for television, although the six million-dollar, Italian-British co-production was later edited down to a two-hour movie for distribution in Europe, much to Burt's disgust. 'The English butchered a perfectly respectable TV movie for release in theatres so they could have a "turnover". It was dreadful.' Lancaster, however, was fortunate to have such a mammoth television undertaking, given that his feature film career was at its nadir. He also claimed a mammoth – for television – salary. And the making of *Moses* removed much of the self-doubt he had gone through in 1974, when he had been overly critical of his own movies and career.

'This business is essentially one of mediocrity,' he said. 'I thought for a while of giving up acting. It may have been a momentary dissatisfaction, which I am working out, but I think we all come to a point where we take a measuring stick and place it against the past. Then the mood passes and I just get on with acting. I've decided that the best way to carry on is just to step out there in front of the camera, read a line, and hope I can get away with it. We change from time to time in the light of experience. I suppose that's called understanding.'

Moses was filmed in Israel, during the Yom Kippur War. While Lancaster continued to fight his private anti-press battle by punching out a papparazzo, he also had the chance to intercede in a real fight between a Palestinian and a Bedouin tribesman in a skirmish at the Dead Sea shore, in which twenty-one people were killed. Lancaster recalled, 'We woke one morning to find tanks moving down the street in front of our hotel. We hung around but there was nothing we could do even if they'd let us work: our Israeli crew and Jewish actors were in the army. We went back to Rome on the day of the armistice and debated whether to move to

Spain or Spanish Morocco. But the armistice seemed to be holding. We went back to Israel.'

Producer Vincenzo Labella wanted real Bedouins to play the Israelites, so he hired them and their camels (at $9.50 per day per person and per camel). The nomadic Bedouins felt confined by the movie location and kept quitting. For the scene in the first chapter of *Moses*, in which the young Moses, starving in the desert, kills and eats his camel, Labella bought a camel from one Bedouin for 2,500 Israeli pounds (about $600), a record price for a Sinai camel. The animal, named Shoushou, became too much of a pet to the film company to be killed. The slaughtering scene was faked, but when Labella tried to sell the camel back to its owner, who would offer only sixty dollars for her, the producer donated her to a zoo, in disgust.

Lancaster found the length of the filming schedule, thirty-two weeks, 'a long trek. I enjoyed playing the role enormously, even though it went on a little too long. I wouldn't want to do it again. TV is murder. There just isn't enough time the way there is on the big screen. All the time you're under constant pressure to get a certain amount of work done each day. You're not as comfortable as when you're making a film. Television is so powerful a thing, and yet I don't really understand it.' He found himself frequently shouting streams of four-letter words over the Sinai dunes, at what he considered the general ineptitude demonstrated by the RAI/ATV-ITC crew filming *Moses*. 'Fit the character,' he explained. 'Moses was an angry man; he used to shout at God: "If these are your chosen people, why do you give them such troubles?" '

He also persisted in his atheism. 'I do not derive any comfort from orthodox religion,' he said. 'Life is to be lived within the limits of your knowledge and within the concept of what you would like to see yourself be. I don't follow any creed apart from realising that man cannot live by swimming pools alone. I'm anti-racist, anti-pollution, anti-war, pro-the poor – and none of the things I want will be achieved in my lifetime. All it has done, this Moses role, is to make me understand religion more. I found myself reading the Bible, something I hadn't done since I was fifteen. I guess it's part of an actor's normal way of working – research – but some of the book must have rubbed off on me.'

The Burgess script, done in collaboration with Italian screenwriter Vittorio Bonicelli (who wrote *The Garden of the Finzi-Continis*), was solid except for a few anachronistic lines like, 'It's this one-God business I find hard to take in'. The cast included Irene Papas as Zipporah, Anthony Quayle as Moses's brother Aaron and Ingrid Thulin as their sister Miriam. Although the five-million-dollar production was filmed in English, it was dubbed into Italian and had its world premiere in a seven-hour version on television in Italy, to great acclaim. Lancaster took the film to England and assisted in its cutting to six forty-eight minute chapters for CBS and ITV. He was understandably miffed when the American network threw it away as a summer replacement; he had understood it would be aired during Easter week. Yet the producer in him somewhat understood the CBS thinking: 'You can see the network point of view – who wants to watch a six–hour religious picture. Can miracles compete with guns and cops. Can *Moses* get the ratings of *Kojak*?'

William Lancaster, then twenty-seven played the young Moses, in Part One. 'I'm proud of him, Billy the Kid,' said Burt. 'I told him it's a tough profession, and you've got to be very lucky. You can work your whole life in it and come out with nothing but memories. I've known people of seventy years of age who have been in lots of little dinky shows and really done nothing. Billy happens to be a very talented actor, even though I don't think he has any desire to be one. He got involved in *Moses* by accident – the producer liked him and thought he'd make a great young Moses. I told Bill, "If you think you're going to be a star and get fame and fortune, forget it! You've got to love the business and accept the fact that maybe you'll never be terribly important. Then, and only then, you've got a chance to be someone, and then you'll love it too." I've let him alone; I don't want to overshadow him. I walked off the set every time he began a scene, and I wouldn't even stay to watch him secretly. He happens to be very bright and intelligent and he knew I was doing the right thing. He's not going to trade on my name.'

In *Gruppo Di Famiglia in Un Iterno (Conversation Piece)*, his second film for Visconti, Lancaster played an ageing American art historian (who had an Italian mother), whose life and ivory-tower apartment in Rome are invaded by a family of 1970s free-living philistines and worse (including Silvana Mangano and Helmut Berger). Dominique Sanda appeared briefly as the professor's mother in a flashback to fifty years before, as an homage to Visconti, who had been very ill. Claudia Cardinale cleared her schedule to make a cameo appearance as the professor's wife, also in flashback, an act of gratitude for Visconti's recovery. Vincent Canby in *The New York Times* called Lancaster's performance 'a formidably intelligent piece of work'.

'Visconti stopped all shooting on *Conversation Piece* because he saw three TV antennae in the distance,' Burt remembered. 'I was getting $50,000 a week overtime and said maybe he should take some of my money back. He didn't approve of that. "I stop shooting so my producers and crew learn I'm serious when I say no antennae. At times like this you must be intransigent." '

After the American success of his *Last Tango in Paris*, Bernardo Bertolucci persuaded the Hollywood studios Paramount, Twentieth Century-Fox and United Artists to combine to put up the six million dollars the director said he needed to make his three-hour movie, *1900*, in exchange for one-third each of the distribution. The movie ended up costing nine million dollars, and running five hours in its full-length version. 'Bertolucci was brilliant,' said Burt, 'but extremely difficult to work with, because every morning we came on the set, every single thing in the shooting schedule had been changed, and we would have to waste three or four hours so the changes could be made. These were conditions I simply wasn't used to.

'Bertolucci was really very naughty. He knew he wasn't going to make the three-hour picture he had contracted for. After all, it's a fifty-year historical perspective of the life of Italy. The script I saw, which was only the first half, concerned only me and the old peasant, Sterling Hayden – it was 180 pages long. Our two grandsons, Robert De Niro and Gerard Depardieu, were still little boys when it ended, so I knew there was going to be another whole movie there. My role is that of a ruthless aristocrat, a man who hates his son but loves his grandson. Eventually, I become old and crusty and senile. One of the scenes that was lifted in Italy because of the censors was where I attempt sexual intimacy with a little girl. In anger, and impotence and shame, I hang myself. It doesn't matter that Bertolucci was naughty, he went ahead and made a marvellous movie: his creation.

'Ever since I saw *Last Tango in Paris* I had wanted to

[164]

work with Bertolucci. When he came to see me we talked and talked; Bertolucci asked me to do *1900*, but there was no way he could meet my usual salary so I worked for nothing. I wasn't doing anything at the time and it was only two weeks' work. So I went to Parma, Italy, right near where Bertolucci was born, and treated the whole thing like a vacation. I found the ageing character I play a very rich, exciting part. There are times, however, when I do a film like *Cassandra Crossing*, simply because I need the money. I kid you not. It's a matter of lifestyle. I have only one dress suit to my name, and a few jackets and pants, but it still costs me $300,000 a year just to live. I must continue to work.

'*The Cassandra Crossing* was a different tickle,' said Lancaster, 'broad kitsch. I worked on it for two weeks and got a lot of money. Not only did I not get to see Poland or the Cassandra Bridge, but I never saw the movie. Though I worked with the director, writing scenes for Richard Harris and Sophia Loren, the script was bad. The director would get mad, yell at everyone, "Hell, Lancaster and I worked our asses off to write these lines for you. You don't like them. Well, I'll let you have the original ones, then see how you like that." Actually, I enjoyed sitting with the marvellous Ingrid Thulin and talking for ten days straight. My best line in that movie was "Listen, why don't you just take the dog for a walk? Hello? Yes. Yes. The train is approaching." '

The Cassandra Crossing was put together by Carlo Ponti and Lew Grade, who with this picture obtained his nickname, Sir Low Grade (late Lord Low Grade). Ponti's wife, Loren, and Ava Gardner were among the passengers exposed to a deadly virus brought on board a Geneva-Stockholm express train by a young terrorist.

[165]

The authorities, headed by Lancaster and Thulin, quarantine the entire train and since no country will admit the train, they divert it to the deserted bridge of the title, which may no longer even exist. This 'disaster movie', climaxed by a train crash, of course, was overshadowed by the real-life drama of Ponti, Loren, Gardner and Harris, who were accused of sneaking art treasures out of Italy during the filming of *The Cassandra Crossing*. They were arraigned by the Italian courts, and Gardner and Harris faced instant arrest if they entered Italy. The case against them was never proved, and eventually dropped, but the Pontis fought what was essentially a tax battle for several more years, ending with a short prison term for Sophia. Lancaster, the most passionate art collector in the bunch, was not involved in any way.

Robert Altman's *Buffalo Bill and the Indians* (or *Sitting Bull's History Lesson*), released in the summer of 1976 for the United States Bicentennial Celebration, was loosely based on Arthur Kopit's unsuccessful Broadway play, *Indians*. Both works satirised the legend of Buffalo Bill, perhaps the first creation of American show business, the first star whose celebrity was not based on prior military, athletic, political or thespian exploits but who was more the creation of publicity and an 'image'. The movie, even more than the play, emphasised the phony show business cowboy as an 1880s substitute for saints and heroes. Buffalo Bill Cody, as played by Paul Newman in his only Altman film, drinks whisky by the barrel, chases deep-diaphragmed opera singers and is afraid of birds. He uses buckshot in his six-shooter, would not know how to track an Indian, and his long golden locks are a wig. But with his travelling Wild West Show, camped for the winter in the movie,

Buffalo Bill is also America's premiere late nineteenth-century entertainer.

Lancaster played Ned Buntline, the dime novelist (aka E. Z. C. Judson) who first immortalised Buffalo Bill in *King of the Border Men* in 1869 and started the Wild West Show in 1883, but is now disenchanted with the legend he has created. He now pokes holes in that legend, along with Chief Sitting Bull (Frank Kaquitts), the show's intransigent star attraction, the Chief's interpretor (Will Sampson) and a testy Indian agent (Denver Pyle). The remainder of the cast, including Altman regular Geraldine Chaplin as Annie Oakley, show producer Nate Salsbury (Joel Grey), publicist John Burke (Kevin McCarthy) and even the President of the United States, Grover Cleveland (Pat McCormick) and First Lady (Shelley Duvall) recognise Cody's fraudulence but are co-conspirators in his public front, for a variety of reasons. *Buffalo Bill and the Indians* also has a strong secondary theme of white exploitation of the Indian.

Although the movie had a screenplay, by Altman and Alan Rudolph (with memorable lines like Cody's 'If I'd had the time I'd a done everything I said I did'), it was filmed in Altman's usual improvisational style, with many of the actors supplying their own dialogue. The director made sure that the outdoor fifteen-tent village set (on Canada's Stoney Indian Reserve) was finished two weeks ahead of the start of filming, so that actors could hang around to soak up the atmosphere they needed. Chaplin played Annie Oakley with her arm in a sling, after falling off a horse while trying to learn to shoot standing up on its back. 'Altman is less restrictive than any director I've ever worked with,' said Newman. 'He demands and depends a great deal on actors outside the confinements and construction of the script. In a way, Buffalo Bill is me – take a look at the magazine interviews that aren't true, the stories that never existed. Playing Buffalo Bill is a very humbling experience . . . he's finally a human being. Heroes, movie stars, can't live up to their own legends. I did use my own background, but there's no way that what you see up on the screen is me.'

Lancaster, as a firm believer in the script who would work as hard as necessary to have it in final form before filming began, was a little lost in Altman's mélange. And since the director never disagreed with anyone – least of all his actors, letting them all talk at once, much like his characters on screen – Burt had no one's (or everyone's) concept of the movie to argue against. It was far from his usual style. However, during the filming of one scene in a sawdust-strewn salon, Lancaster as Buntline stood next to the bar piled high with peanut shells, telling some particularly malicious stories about Buffalo Bill's clawing his way to success. At the end of the take, Burt pulled the pipe from his mouth, made a startled face and mouthed the single word 'good'.

While *Buffalo Bill and the Indians* met with mostly critical hostility (and non-existent box office), Jack Kroll in *Newsweek* called it an 'ambitious, impudent, brainy, sorrowfully funny movie'. David Sterritt, in *The Christian Science Monitor*, said that Lancaster as Ned Buntline 'gives his most moving performance in quite a while'.

Lancaster filmed the re-make of H. G. Wells' *The Island of Dr Moreau* in the Virgin Islands in 1976-77. As Charles Laughton had in the early 1930s, he played the genius whose genetic experiments produce creatures that are half animal and half human, or 'humanimals', as they were termed by John Chambers and Dan Striepke, who created them and the creatures in the

Planet of the Apes movies. The Laughton version had run into censorship problems because of its suggestion of bestiality.

'This one is different,' said Lancaster. 'I am playing Dr Moreau as a dedicated scientist who, before he goes mad, feels that what he is doing is a noble thing. He believes it is the duty of science to investigate all things. But look what happens when it does. God knows what is going on today in the bowels of those government laboratories. Theoretically it is possible for science to create superior people, but who is to determine this superiority? Where shall the seat of that God-like power be? I'm not afraid of playing ageing heroic characters, although I don't think Dr Moreau is a heroic character. What we tried to do was play him as – what can I say? – obviously an unusual man, a man involved in his career, a strange man. So we played him dead straight on.'

Bill Lancaster did find fame and fortune in Hollywood after all, in 1976, at the age of twenty-eight and as a screenwriter, which made his father doubly proud. Bill was paid $750,000 for his original script *The Bad News Bears*, a critical and commercial success about a Little League baseball team who become contenders with the help of a tomboy pitcher (Tatum O'Neal) and a drunken coach (Walter Matthau).

Billy, who had considered himself 'a rich Hollywood kid' and a misfit because of his leg crippled by polio, flunked out of high school. 'I had more interesting things to do.' He returned to finish school, but after a brief pass at junior college found a job reading movie scripts. The first three scripts he wrote with a friend went unbought, but *Bears*, submitted on speculation, was picked up by Paramount, which hired him to do two more pictures (*The Thing* re-make was one of them).

'You've got to persevere,' Bill Lancaster said. Married at eighteen, and divorced, with a ten-year-old daughter who did not pitch baseballs, he lived alone in an apartment in Beverly Hills, his brief acting career behind him forever.

By 1977, Burt Lancaster's lack of bankability and choice of subject matter were such that he was forced to spend some $150,000 of his own money, an unprecedented investment, in *Go Tell the Spartans*, an anti-war movie that he felt was the best project offered to him in several years. He was concerned that American audiences would not accept this story in which he played an unconventional major leading his young troops through the blood and mud of the Vietnam War. 'It's extremely difficult for Americans to accept the idea that they can be beaten in any way,' he said. 'Nobody else would put any money into our film. It was a struggle for us to bring it out. But what we finally achieved was excellent. I'm very pleased with it, and very proud of it.'

Lancaster insisted on doing most of the slogging stuntwork in *Go Tell the Spartans* himself, despite recently having had an operation for recurring knee trouble, the belated legacy of his acrobatic career.

In *Twilight's Last Gleaming*, Lancaster played a former US Air Force General serving a life sentence for murder; he escapes and finds his way into an American atomic missile base. He threatens to launch an atomic holocaust unless his demands are met by the President. This topical thriller was directed by Robert Aldrich, who was the hiring boss this time. Lancaster's co-conspirators were played by Paul Winfield, Charles Durning and Burt Young, with Richard Widmark playing the 'good' general, to whom the problem is given. 'Bob Aldrich is a sweetheart and I love him,' said Burt. 'I've made four films with him and I confess I was disappointed in *Last Gleaming*. I think there were good things in it we didn't quite bring out.'

In 1978, Lancaster donated one of his most important paintings to the Los Angeles County Art Museum, Thomas Hart Benton's 'The Kentuckian', a five-by-seven-foot canvas of Burt in the title part of his 1955 film, which had been shot in 1954. The painting by Benton (1889-1975), had been in a warehouse since then. Lancaster had previously given a Henri Rousseau naif-style painting to the LA County Museum. At the ceremony turning over 'The Kentuckian', the museum's director noted, 'it's rare to have the patron, donor and subject on hand at a presentation.'

In 1979, when Cliff Robertson took himself out of the running for President of the Screen Actors Guild, Lancaster was approached to run for the office. He considered it, but as president and eighty per cent owner of Norlan Productions, theoretically at least an employer of actors, he was ineligible. Norlan was the remains of his production companies, ranging from Norma through Hecht-Hill-Lancaster, and had produced nothing for a while. There was one property in development, however, and Burt decided not to divest himself of the company in order to head SAG.

In January of 1980, Lancaster entered Cedars-Sinai Hospital in Los Angeles for an eleven-hour 'intricate abdominal surgery'. He was on the critical list, but his spokesman emphasised that his sudden ill health was 'not cancer-related'. The operation turned out to be a tricky gall bladder removal, and briefly put him in unusual danger.

In August of 1981, Lancaster and Kirk Douglas finally got their wish to work together in a comedy, but on stage rather than in films. *The Boys of Autumn* was a

[171]

fanciful telling of what happened in later life to Tom Sawyer and Huckleberry Finn, by a Chicago college professor, Bernard Sabath. Tom (Douglas) and Huck (Lancaster), in their sixties, were on stage for the whole of the one-set play. 'We meet on a hill overlooking the Mississippi,' Douglas recalled, 'and at first I don't know him – after all it's been a long time. Then we sit down to talk about our lives. We've both done things we're unhappy about. He confesses to the mercy killing of his wife. I've been a child molester. There it is.'

'Aren't we too rich for this?' asked Douglas of Lancaster after another twelve-hour rehearsal for the play, in San Francisco.

'Neither one of us is used to such hard work,' said Lancaster, who lost the coin toss up for top billing. 'But working in a play like this we've learned a lot about each other. The show was a hit, and we could have gone on doing it as a sort of personal appearance in a number of theatres. But both of us knew it wasn't good enough, and it was damned hard work. I was relieved when we agreed that it was too exhausting. I much prefer film.'

In 1981, Lancaster also returned to Italy to make *La Pelle (The Skin)*, for director Liliana Cavani. He played General Mark Clark in this story of the Allied occupation of Naples during World War II, and co-starred with Claudia Cardinale for the fourth time. Marcello Mastroianni was also in the cast. The movie was given no major release in England or America. Almost equally ignored, although it was an American movie, was *Cattle Annie and Little Britches*, about two teenaged girls from the east (Amanda Plummer and Diane Lane) who visit the Old West in its dying days looking for adventure. Lancaster, Scott Glenn and John Savage, as members of the Doolin-Dalton gang, provide that adventure, along

with Rod Steiger as the villain. 'In this world of piss-
ants and grovellers . . .' begins one of Burt's speeches,
in this infectiously sentimental mock-Western that
Universal dumped on the market unceremoniously,
leaving *Cattle Annie and Little Britches* to find its audience in revival houses and on cable television.

CHAPTER THIRTEEN

Local Hero

IN LOUIS MALLE'S *Atlantic City*, Lancaster had a new challenge. 'I've never tried anything like this – a weak character,' he said. 'It's good to reach out to try something different.' In John Guare's original screenplay, Burt played a white-haired, ex-gangland bagman, Lou, who has lived in the New Jersey resort city for forty years, long enough to remember when 'the Atlantic Ocean was really something'. He only briefly strikes it rich after gambling becomes legal in 1978. Lou now runs errands for his bedridden landlady and sometime lover (Kate Reid) and becomes fascinated by his young neighbour (Susan Sarandon) whose aspiration is to become Monte Carlo's first female croupier. On the set of *Atlantic City*, Sarandon found her co-star 'thoroughly professional, and accessible, although he didn't hang out'.

Lancaster won every major award it was possible to win for *Atlantic City*, except the Oscar. Burt received the Best Actor Award from the New York Critics (for the fourth time), the National Society of Film Critics, the Los Angeles Film Critics Association, and the British Film and Television Academy. When Henry Fonda beat him out for Best Actor at the American Academy Awards (for *On Golden Pond*), Lancaster said, 'I'm glad he got it. First of all, it was a wonderful performance. Secondly, after forty years . . . .'

In accepting his own Best Actor Award for *Atlantic City* from Los Angeles Film Critics Association, Lancaster pointed out that the movie had been something less than a box office smash hit. 'Maybe the award will help,' he said, 'for apart from myself, Kirk Douglas and my immediate family, I don't think anyone else has seen the picture.'

To play the ageing Pope Gregory X in *Marco Polo* in 1982, for America's NBC-TV and Italy's RAI, Lancaster again acted partly with his hair. Coming off the paunchy, slope-shouldered and white-haired has-been in *Atlantic City*, he was unselfconscious about putting curlers in his now naturally cinnamon-and-sugar hair to portray Gregory. The mini-series *Marco Polo* was budgeted at between twelve and thirteen million dollars, but ended up costing thirty million. Much of it was filmed in mainland China, but Lancaster's part as the medieval Pope Gregory was filmed in Rome, in both Italian and English. This meant that Burt could live at his other home, an old and spacious apartment near the Trevi Fountain.

Lancaster had owned the apartment for twelve years by then, but of course his involvement with Italy went back much further than that. 'I love opera, pasta and the sound of laughter, so it figures that I'd love Italy,' he told writer George Christy. Burt recalled his wartime years in the country, and that *The Crimson Pirate* had been made on the island of Ischia, off the Bay of Naples, before anyone outside of the country had heard of it.

'It's much more beautiful than Capri,' he said, 'now of course it's become the fashionable place to go.' By the time of *The Leopard* he was speaking Italian well enough to consider living in Italy, 'so I decided it would be comfortable to have a residence in Rome as well as in California. Rome is convenient for the family, and my youngest daughter, Sighle, spends a considerable amount of time there now.'

Because the apartment is located in Rome's historic district, 'we couldn't do anything to the outside; you're forbidden to make any exterior changes that will alter the look of antiquity, even to adding a balcony or an extra room.' But Lancaster redid the interior of the flat, using Roman artisans, except for the library, where he used designer Jim Vance, of Carmel, California, who had been artistic director for movies done by Robert Aldrich and Robert Altman. 'The pillows in the bedroom are covered with a glazed Italian silk in soft muted colours; they were designed for me by Enrico Sabbatini, who created the costumes for the *Marco Polo* mini-series. But the only movie memorabilia that I have displayed in the apartment is a huge blow-up of me from *The Leopard* – in it I'm dancing with Claudia Cardinale.'

The back wall of his bedroom, behind the bed, was taken over by a hand-sewn hanging depicting a classical view of Rome, by the Italian artist Maria Teresa Capodanno. Lancaster added valuable Turkish rugs to the floor of his bedroom: 'I bought them in an open-air bazaar in Istanbul years ago.' He displayed three paintings by another Italian artist, Lorenzo Tornabuoni, in the entrance hall, library and guest room. 'I heard about Tornabouni through the artist Guttoso, whose art commands high prices,' said Lancaster. 'Tornabuoni is relatively new, and it's exciting to discover another artist that I like, believe in and care to collect.'

Lancaster was particularly pleased with his dining-room table in Rome, which he came upon by accident in a furniture workroom, where it was being built for another client. 'This was the perfect look,' he said, 'a strong design of black-enamelled wood, with inlays of brass, and brass legs. It accommodates six or eight, which is my ideal number for a dinner party. I like to cook and entertain when I'm in Italy. I've mastered the skill of preparing pasta, which so many Americans ruin by overcooking, and all of my sauces are authentic, whether I'm serving spaghetti *carbonara* or *matriciana*. I grow my own herbs – basil, rosemary and oregano – just as the Italians do, and I plant flowers in between, which is an Italian custom. There's a huge market in Rome, the size of two Twentieth Century-Fox sound stages, that's filled with flowers. I buy them there at half the price I would have to pay at a fancy flower shop.'

At home in Rome, he relaxed by reading or listening to his large collection of classical and opera records. 'Deep down, I'm a frustrated opera singer,' he reminded. 'I also like to hole up in the library and read. There's always a film script that must be read, but I like to re-read Plato, Aristotle, Dreiser, Hemingway, Faulkner, Wolfe. I never tire of reading the classics, or going to concerts to hear fine symphonic or chamber music. If there's an empty space on my shelves occasionally, it's because I love to give albums to people who appreciate music; that's why my record library is rarely complete.'

Lancaster also enjoyed living in Los Angeles, but paradoxically preferred condominiums in Century City as both residence and office. He kept a beach house in

Malibu, but rarely went there, considering it 'too far to drive'. He continued to show up at the office in jogging suits, usually blue, sometimes wearing a battered hat and a hand-woven Mexican Indian shawl, a *quechquemitl*, and carrying a worn leather mail pouch bulging with movie scripts. He still chainsmoked unfiltered Camel cigarettes, a nearly life-long habit. 'I know, I live in a land full of health nuts,' he said, 'and I still smoke. But I run everyday to offset the effect. I also love living in California, although I'm one of the few actors who live in a high-rise apartment. I go to the office every day to talk to writers and read scripts. If I do nothing else, I read and read and read. In a funny way, I work harder here than when I'm making a movie.'

In October of 1982, Lancaster volunteered to narrate a half-hour television commercial attacking the so-called Moral Majority and similar right-wing groups for their 'political intolerance reminiscent of witch hunts, slavery and McCarthyism'. The commercial, which was prepared by television producer Norman Lear's organisation, People for the American Way, at a cost of $200,000, was aired in major cities throughout America during the month. As narrator, Lancaster said at the beginning of the programme, 'You'll see that we, as a nation, are besieged today by a powerful wealthy movement with one dangerous goal.' The narrative never mentioned the Moral Majority by name, but a spokesman for that group, Cal Thomas, said the commercial was 'a total piece of blatant propaganda' that took Moral Majority positions out of context.

Lancaster finally got to do his screen comedy in 1983. *Local Hero*, a relatively low-budget British movie, was David Puttnam's first as a producer after his Oscar-winning *Chariots of Fire*. It was writer-director Bill Forsyth's first work after he won the British Academy

Award for his screenplay for *Gregory's Girl*. Forsyth felt that he had at first unconsciously written the character of Felix Happer, an eccentric Houston oil millionaire, with Lancaster in mind. 'In my head I began to hear him saying the dialogue,' said Forsyth. 'Then I think I started writing it especially for him. Of course it was amazing when he read the script and was interested in doing it.'

'It was the best script I'd received since *Atlantic City*,' said Lancaster, 'a good part in a good script, it's as simple as that. What's nice is that there are no villains, just eccentrics. It's like those lovely old Ealing movies.' Of Forsyth, he said, 'There'll be no stopping that young man.' Of his own character he noted, 'Felix Happer is just a little mad. When he's not putting his business rivals literally over a barrel, he's shoring up his psyche with "abuse therapy", or indulging his passion for astronomy. His office is a private planetarium, with a "star" projector and a telescope NASA would envy. Then again, everyone in this movie is a little strange, but that's the charm of Forsyth's script. He is a superb writer on the frailties of human nature.'

Forsyth kiddingly described *Local Hero* as 'a combination of *Apocalypse Now* and *Brigadoon*'. For all of his lovable foibles, Lancaster's Happer wants even more oil than he has, and looks to the North Sea to get it. He dispatches a young associate (Peter Riegert), a 'telex man' from the oil company's Mergers and Acquisitions department, to the small Scottish fishing village of Ferness. The young man's job is to convince the locals to sell Happer the whole village and, not incidentally, to keep an eye on the constellation Virgo for Happer from this superior vantage point. The villagers offer little resistance to the American plan, but pretend to be reluctant to drive up the price. Meanwhile a pretty young marine biologist (Jenny Seagrove) further complicates the issue by believing that the American, and the village pub owner and chief negotiator for the locals (Denis Lawson), are planning to turn the area over to a marine research station instead of an oilfield.

The comic twist comes when Riegert's character becomes increasingly convinced that the idyllic setting should not be turned over to petroleum exploration, while the natives become even more convinced that they should sell out at a high price. Happer is forced to fly over from Houston to take up the negotiations.

Producer Puttnam got the idea from a newspaper clipping about a Scotsman who had sold his private island to an American oil company. 'It was a fantastic deal,' he recalled, 'full of penalty clauses, profit sharing, deferred payments, the works. I wondered how rural Scots and the Texas oil men would get along. Somewhere in there was the idea for the movie, but it needed a gentle comic approach, the sort of thing Frank Capra and Preston Sturges did so well. Few film makers have that touch in this day of going for the big laugh.'

Lancaster said, 'One of the privileges of being my age is that you get to choose the roles you like; when a good script comes along, like this one, I get the urge to go back to work. Forsyth never puts his characters down, he indulges them and treats their failings with affectionate humour. This was a very difficult part to play, as the character is sort of half mad. When you try to play a character like this you don't know how far to take it, because it's meant to be humorous. You've got to be careful that you don't farcialise it, play it overboard, play it too big, which is the temptation, rather than let the total effect of what is happening affect an attitude of charm and mirth. You want to go

[181]

in and punch it up, and that's very dangerous with Forsyth's kind of writing.'

Burt only spent two weeks filming his part in *Local Hero*, but managed to spend some of his time in Scotland, in the Highlands near Inverness, trout fishing in a stream near Inverlochy Castle, and standing his rounds of pints of brown ale at the pubs. He indulged fans who asked for autographs, or for him to sign faded old stills from his classic films ('my baby pictures'). He recalled one such pub visit with locals, where, with bagpipes blaring in the background, 'one of them kept asking me about *Birdman of Alcatraz* as if it had been released just yesterday.'

On the Houston location, Lancaster's old directorial instincts surfaced, but in much milder form than in previous decades. Forsyth recalled shooting Lancaster's first scene in Texas, in which he has to push through a line of policemen to get to his limousine. 'We had real cops,' said the director, 'who were a bit timid of Lancaster. He was supposed to barge through and part them, and they backed off. I said to them to allow Burt to push through and went back to the camera where I saw him talking to them, and I thought, "He's going to be OK, he's helping out." He was just saying the same thing to them in American. He saw me seeing him do this, and before he went back to his mark he came over to the camera and said, "I hope you don't mind me talking to the other performers but I thought I could help". I said he could do it whenever he liked.'

Local Hero was an instant hit on its London release, and a critical if not commercial success in America. *Time* said that Lancaster was 'expertly doing his clean-old-man routine', and that Forsyth was a 'shrewd film maker worth bending near so you can hear what he has to say amidst the contemporary din'. The *Hollywood*

[182]

Reporter called *Local Hero* 'a quaint, sardonic and laudably unpretentious film. It often shines as brilliantly as the Northern skies which lume its background . . . There are no villains, no saints in this fine, intelligent production, only people.'

The Osterman Weekend, Lancaster's second movie of 1983, was clearly the alternate one he did only for the money. Based on Robert Ludlum's thriller of the same name, the first Ludlum book to be made into a movie, *The Osterman Weekend* told the confusing, extremely violent and improbable story of a weekend at the country home of an American television interviewer (Rutger Hauer). Hauer has been convinced by a CIA man (John Hurt) that the three close friends who are visiting him for the weekend are Soviet spies. Lancaster plays the CIA chief who wants to be President, and sanctions Hurt's recruiting Hauer to allow the agency to spy on his chums. Lancaster is grimly believable in his few scenes as the CIA head, but director Sam Peckinpah's first movie in five years was notable only for its violent excesses.

In May of 1983, Burt took a brief vacation on Kapalua Bay on the Hawaiian island of Maui. He was resting up for a planned role opposite Broadway's Raul Julia *(Nine)* in a homosexually-themed story ('it's more love', said Lancaster), *The Kiss of the Spider Woman.* Based on the novel by Manuel Puig, *The Kiss of the Spider Woman* was to have been directed by Hector Babenco *(Pixote)* in Paris and Brazil, but fell apart, temporarily. By the time *Kiss* was finally reset to begin in Brazil in October, Lancaster had had his heart surgery and was set for *Firestarter.* William Hurt was signed opposite Raul Julia for *The Kiss of the Spider Woman.*

In the summer of 1983, two months before the release of *The Osterman Weekend,* Lancaster entered Cedars (of

[183]

Lebanon)-(Mount) Sinai Hospital in Los Angeles for tests and observation; it was determined by his doctors, after discovering blockages in his coronary arteries, that he needed a quadruple bypass operation as soon as his heart muscles were strong enough to withstand the surgery. Once he knew of the possibility of such surgery, Burt resumed his 'training' so that his body would be ready for it. Possibly as a result of these fitness efforts, his five-and-a-half-hour surgery went 'incredibly well', according to his secretary Sandy Wiesenthal. The first morning after the operation, he was up reading the newspaper. 'They told me the only other one who did that was George Burns,' he laughed. He was moved out of intensive care into a private room only three days after the operation, was walking the halls the next day, and left Cedars-Sinai only ten days after he first went in for surgery. Four days after that he was working out on the track. He was expected to resume working, in the film *Firestarter* a month after leaving the hospital.

Lancaster did have to resign from two previously announced projects: *Maria's Lovers*, with Nastassia Kinski and John Savage, and *AD*, an NBC-TV mini-series, starring Julie Christie and Sada Thompson. He had been looking forward to both films, especially to working with Kinski. In *Maria's Lovers*, Soviet director Andrei Konchalovsky's first American movie, in which Lancaster would have played Savage's father, he was replaced by Robert Mitchum. In *AD* which deals with the effect of Christianity on the Roman Empire in the years 30-69 AD, Lancaster was replaced in the role of the Emperor Tiberius by James Mason. Despite his earlier misgivings about the release of *Moses*, Burt had been eager to work again with Anthony Burgess, who also wrote the script for *AD*, along with producer Vincenzo

Labella. But a seven-month shooting schedule in Tunisia, the site of Labella's earlier mini-series *Jesus of Nazareth*, followed by two more months in Rome, Pompeii and Herculaneum, was deemed too gruelling for a recent heart patient, even one of Burt's constitution.

He was supposed to return to work by 14 October 1983, in Dino DiLaurentiis's *Firestarter*, on its Wilmington, North Carolina location. *Firestarter* also starred Drew Barrymore in the title part. However, Lancaster was required on location even earlier than the announced start date, and his doctors forbade the trip and the exertion of filming. His part was re-written for Martin Sheen.

'I feel great,' said Lancaster at the time of the operation. 'I've been leading the life of a saint: no smoking, no drinking, no sex.' He paused, then said, 'I cheat a little.'

Jackie Bone, his girlfriend of seventeen years, was still very much in evidence, but there were still no marriage plans. 'She hasn't yelled for it yet,' Lancaster said.

The Leopard was re-released in September of 1983, in its uncut, 185-minute Italian-language version, in which the star is dubbed. Lancaster again pronounced it 'A wonderful, lovely movie' – in either language: 'The English version as far as I'm concerned is good too.' He was amused at the revisionist body of criticism that had grown up around him and *The Leopard* in the two decades since its initial release. 'When *The Leopard* first came out,' he recalled, 'it got good reviews, but the critics laughed at me. I was a bum. Twenty years later they're saying, "It's his *chef d'oeuvre*, his great acting piece." I don't know what happened to these people, but suddenly I've become a hell of a performer.'

[185]

Lancaster, of course, had always felt confident about his acting, given the right screenplay, director and other surrounding circumstances. But what he had learned in his seventy years was that, while he planned always to remain active, he no longer needed to act, 'unless I find a piece of work that really excites me. You've no idea the rubbish that's sent to me. Tits and sand; that's what we used to call sex and violence in Hollywood.' He had also calmed down a lot in seven decades: 'I don't have the energy to be explosive,' he said.

'Getting older means you have to keep your mind open, try new things. Some of us finally realise that maturity means consideration for other people. I think it is the ability to love yourself and consequently others. I know now it's not necessary to go through life being a warrior. I've jumped through too many windows in the past, and I'm no longer young Lochinvar sweeping in from the West. It's something everybody has to go through, getting older. But I won't retire. That's death. I'll always find something to occupy myself. It's exciting. It's a new ball game every day.'

Filmography

1946
1. *The Killers*. Universal (Mark Hellinger). Director: Robert Siodmak. Screenplay: Anthony Veiller, based on the short story by Ernest Hemingway. Cast also included: Ava Gardner, Edmond O'Brien, Albert Dekker, Sam Levene, Jeff Corey, William Conrad. Remade in 1964 by Universal, with Don Siegel directing and John Cassavetes in Lancaster's role of 'The Swede'.

1947
2. *Desert Fury*. Paramount (Hal Wallis). Lewis Allen. Robert Rossen, based on the novel by Ramona Stewart. Cast: John Hodiak, Lizabeth Scott, Wendell Corey (film debut), Mary Astor. Colour.
3. *Brute Force*. Universal (Mark Hellinger). Jules Dassin. Richard Brooks, based on the story by Robert Patterson. Cast: Hume Cronyn, Charles Bickford, Yvonne De Carlo, Ann Blyth, Ella Raines, Anita Colby, Sam Levene, Howard Duff, Jeff Corey.
4. *Variety Girl*. Paramount. George Marshall. Edmund

Hartmann, Frank Tashlin, Robert Welch and Monte Brice. Cast: Olga San Juan, Mary Hatcher, De Forest Kelley, William Demarest and guest stars, including Bing Crosby, Bob Hope, William Holden, Lizabeth Scott, Robert Preston, Veronica Lake, Sterling Hayden, Macdonald Carey.

1948
5. *I Walk Alone*. Paramount (Hal Wallis). Byron Haskin. Charles Schnee, based on the play *Beggers Are Coming to Town*, by Theodore Reeves, adapted by Robert Smith and John Bright. Cast: Lizabeth Scott, Kirk Douglas, Wendell Corey.
6. *All My Sons*. Universal. Irving Reis. Chester Erskine, based on the play by Arthur Miller. Cast: Edward G. Robinson, Mady Christians, Louisa Horton, Howard Duff, Frank Conroy, Arlene Francis.
7. *Sorry, Wrong Number*. Paramount (Hal Wallis). Anatole Litvak. Lucille Fletcher, based on her own radio play. Cast: Barbara Stanwyck, Ann Richards, Wendell Corey, Ed Begley, Lief Erickson, William Conrad. Stanwyck was nominated for the Best Actress Oscar.
8. *Kiss the Blood Off My Hands*. Universal. Norman Foster. Eric Bercovici, based on the novel by Gerald Butler, adapted by Ben Maddow and Walter Bernstein. Cast: Joan Fontaine, Robert Newton, Lewis Russell. Lancaster's first movie as a producer (with Harold Hecht), under the Norma production company.

1949
9. *Criss Cross*. Universal. Robert Siodmak. Daniel Fuchs, based on the novel by Don Tracy. Cast: Yvonne De Carlo, Dan Duryea, Stephen McNally, Richard Long.

10. *Rope of Sand.* Paramount (Hal Wallis). William Dieterle. Walter Doniger, additional dialogue by John Paxton. Cast: Paul Henreid, Claude Rains, Corinne Calvet, Peter Lorre, Sam Jaffe.

1950

11. *The Flame and the Arrow.* Warner Brothers (Hecht-Norma). Jacques Tourneur. Waldo Salt. Cast: Virginia Mayo, Robert Douglas, Aline MacMahon, Frank Allenby, Nick Cravat. Colour.

12. *Mister 880.* Twentieth Century-Fox. Edmund Goulding. Robert Riskin, based on articles by St Clair McKelway. Cast: Dorothy McGuire, Edmund Gwenn. Gwenn was nominated for the Best Supporting Actor Academy Award.

1951

13. *Vengeance Valley.* Metro-Goldwyn-Mayer. Richard Thorpe. Irving Ravetch, based on the story by Luke Short. Cast: Robert Walker, Joanne Dru, Sally Forrest, John Ireland, Carleton Carpenter, Ray Collins, Hugh O'Brian. Colour.

14. *Jim Thorpe – All American.* Warner Brothers. Michael Curtiz. Douglas Morrow and Everett Freeman, based on the story by Morrow and Vincent X. Flaherty, and the autobiography by Jim Thorpe and Russell J. Birdwell. Cast: Charles Bickford, Phyllis Thaxter, Steve Cochran, Dick Wesson.

15. *Ten Tall Men.* Columbia (Hecht-Norma). Willis Goldbeck. Roland Kibbee and Frank Davis, based on the story by James Warner Bellah and Goldbeck. Cast: Jody Lawrence, Gilbert Roland, Kieren Moore, George Tobias, Mari Blanchard. Colour.

1952

16. *The Crimson Pirate*. Warner Brothers (Hecht-Norma). Robert Siodmak. Roland Kibbee. Cast: Eva Bartok, Nick Cravat, Margo Grahame, Christopher Lee, Dagmar (later Dana) Wynter, Frank Pettingill. Colour.

17. *Come Back, Little Sheba*. Paramount (Hal Wallis). Daniel Mann. Ketti Frings, based on the play by William Inge. Cast: Shirley Booth, Terry Moore, Richard Jaeckel, Philip Ober. Booth won Oscar as Best Actress. Moore was nominated as Best Supporting Actress.

1953

18. *South Sea Woman*. Warner Brothers. Arthur Lubin. Edwin Blum, based on the play by William M. Rankin, adapted by Earl Baldwin and Stanley Shapiro. Cast: Virginia Mayo, Chuck Connors, Arthur Sheilds, Veola Vonn, Paul Burke.

19. *From Here to Eternity*. Columbia. Fred Zinnemann. Daniel Taradash, based on the novel by James Jones. Cast: Deborah Kerr, Montgomery Clift, Donna Reed, Frank Sinatra, Philip Ober, Ernest Borgnine, Jack Warden. Lancaster won the New York Film Critics Award as Best Actor, and received an Academy Award nomination. Oscars were given to Reed and Sinatra for their supporting roles, to Taradash for his screenplay and to Zinnemann for direction. *From Here to Eternity* was nominated for a total of eleven Academy Awards and won eight.

20. *Three Sailors and a Girl*. Warner Brothers. Roy Del Ruth. Roland Kibbee and Devery Freeman, from a play by George S. Kaufman. Cast: Jane Powell, Gordon MacRae, Gene Nelson, Sam Levene, Jack E. Leonard, Veda Ann Borg. Colour.

1954

21. *His Majesty O'Keefe*. Warner Brothers (Hecht-Norma). Byron Haskin. Borden Chase and James Hill, based on the novel by Lawrence Kingman and Gerald Green. Cast: Joan Rice, Andre Morell, Benson Fong, Tessa Prendergast. Colour.

22. *Apache*. Hecht-Lancaster, released by United Artists. Robert Aldrich. James R. Webb, based on the novel by Paul I. Wellman. Cast: Jean Peters, John McIntire, Charles Buchinsky (later Bronson). Colour.

23. *Vera Cruz*. Hecht-Lancaster, United Artists. Robert Aldrich. Roland Kibbee and James R. Webb, based on a story by Borden Chase. Cast: Gary Cooper, Denise Darcel, Cesar Romero, Ernest Borgnine, Jack Elam. Colour.

1955

24. *The Kentuckian*. Hecht-Lancaster, United Artists. Burt Lancaster. A. B. Guthrie, Jnr, based on the novel by Felix Holt. Cast: Diana Lynn, Dianne Foster, John McIntire, Una Merkel, John Carradine and introducing Walter Matthau. Colour.

25. *The Rose Tattoo*. Paramount. Daniel Mann. Tennessee Williams, based on his own stage play, with adaptation by Hal Kanter. Cast: Anna Magnani, Marisa Pavan, Ben Cooper, Virginia Grey, Jo Van Fleet. Magnani won Best Actress Oscar, and Oscars went to cinematographer James Wong Howe, and a team of four for best black and white art direction/set decoration. *The Rose Tattoo* was nominated as Best Picture but lost to Hecht and Lancaster's own *Marty*.

1956

26. *Trapeze*. Susan Productions, produced by James Hill, released by United Artists. Carol Reed. James R.

Webb, with an adaptation by Liam O'Brien, based on *The Killing Frost* by Max Catto. Cast: Tony Curtis, Gina Lollobrigida, Katy Jurado, John Puleo. Colour. Video available.

27. *The Rainmaker*. Paramount (Hal Wallis). Joseph Anthony. N. Richard Nash, based on his own play. Cast: Katharine Hepburn, Wendell Corey, Lloyd Bridges, Earl Holliman, Cameron Prud'homme. Colour.

1957

28. *Gunfight at the OK Corral*. Paramount (Hal Wallis). John Sturges. Leon Uris, based on the article *The Killer*, by George Scullin. Cast: Kirk Douglas, Rhonda Fleming, Jo Van Fleet, John Ireland, Frank Faylen, Earl Holliman, Lyle Bettger, Dennis Hopper. Colour.

29. *Sweet Smell of Success*. Hecht-Hill-Lancaster, released by United Artists. Alexander MacKendrick. Clifford Odets and Ernest Lehman, based on the novelette by Lehman. Cast: Tony Curtis, Susan Harrison, Martin Milner, Sam Levene, Barbara Nichols, Jeff Donnell, Lurene Tuttle, Edith Atwater, Queenie Smith.

1958

30. *Run Silent, Run Deep*. Hecht-Hill-Lancaster, released by United Artists. Robert Wise. John Gay, based on the novel by Edward L. Beach. Cast: Clark Gable, Jack Warden, Brad Dexter, Don Rickles, Nick Cravat, Eddie Foy III.

31. *Separate Tables*. Hecht-Hill-Lancaster, released by United Artists. Delbert Mann. Terence Rattigan and John Gay, based on Rattigan's play. Cast: Rita Hayworth, Deborah Kerr, David Niven, Wendy Hiller, Gladys Cooper, Cathleen Nesbitt, Rod Taylor. Best Actor Oscar to Niven, Supporting Actress Oscar to

Hiller. Kerr was nominated as Best Actress, and *Separate Tables* for Best Picture.

1959

32. *The Devil's Disciple*. Bryanprod SA and Hecht-Hill-Lancaster (United Artists). Guy Hamilton. John Dighton and Roland Kibbee, based on the play by George Bernard Shaw. Cast: Kirk Douglas, Laurence Olivier, Eva Le Galliene, Harry Andrews, Basil Sydney, George Rose, Janette Scott, Neil McCallum.

1960

33. *The Unforgiven*. Hecht-Hill-Lancaster (United Artists). John Huston. Ben Maddow, based on the novel by Alan LeMay. Cast: Audrey Hepburn, Lillian Gish, Audie Murphy, John Saxon, Charles Bickford, Albert Salmi, Joseph Wiseman. Colour.
34. *Elmer Gantry*. Bernard Smith Production (United Artists). Richard Brooks. Richard Brooks, based on the novel by Sinclair Lewis. Cast: Jean Simmons, Arthur Kennedy, Shirley Jones, Dean Jagger, Patti Page, Edward Andrews, Philip Ober, Rex Ingram. Lancaster won his second New York Film Critics Best Actor Award, and the Oscar. Jones won the Supporting Actress Oscar and Richard Brooks the Oscar for Best Screenplay. Colour.

1961

35. *The Young Savages*. Harold Hecht (United Artists). John Frankenheimer. Edward Anhalt and J. P. Miller, based on the novel by Evan Hunter. Cast: Dina Merrill, Shelley Winters, Edward Andrews, Telly Savalas, Milton Selzer.
36. *Judgment at Nuremberg*. Stanley Kramer Production (United Artists). Stanley Kramer. Abby Mann, based

[193]

on his television play. Cast: Spencer Tracy, Richard Widmark, Marlene Dietrich, Maximilian Schell, Judy Garland, Montgomery Clift, Werner Klemperer, William Shatner. Schell won the Best Actor Oscar. Mann won the Oscar for Best Screenplay. Tracy was nominated as Best Actor and Clift and Garland were nominated for supporting awards. Kramer was nominated as Best Director and *Judgment at Nuremberg* was a candidate for Best Picture.

1962
37. *Birdman of Alcatraz.* Hecht-Hill-Lancaster (United Artists). John Frankenheimer. Guy Trosper, based on the book by Thomas E. Gaddis. Cast: Karl Malden, Thelma Ritter, Betty Field, Edmond O'Brien, Telly Savalas, Whit Bissell. Lancaster won his third New York Film Critics Award as Best Actor, and was nominated for an Oscar. Ritter and Savalas were nominated for supporting awards.

1963
38. *A Child Is Waiting.* Stanley Kramer-Philip Langner Production (United Artists). John Cassavetes. Abby Mann, based on his *Studio One* television play. Cast: Judy Garland, Gena Rowlands, Steven Hill, Elizabeth Wilson.
39. *The List of Adrian Messenger.* Universal. John Huston. Anthony Veiller, based on the novel by Philip MacDonald. Cast: Kirk Douglas, George C. Scott, Tony Curtis, Frank Sinatra, Robert Mitchum, Dana Wynter, Gladys Cooper, Herbert Marshall, John Merivale, John Huston.
40. *(Il Gattopardo) The Leopard.* Titanus/20th Century-Fox. Luchino Visconti. Suso Checchi D'Amico, Pasquale Festa Campanile, Massimo Franciosa, Enrico

Medioli and Luchino Visconti, based on the novel by Giuseppe Lampedusa. Cast: Claudia Cardinale, Alain Delon, Rina Morelli, Romolo Valli. Score by Nino Rota. Colour. Re-released in Italian, 1983.

1964
41. *Seven Days in May.* Paramount. John Frankenheimer. Rod Serling, based on the novel by Fletcher Knebel and Charles W. Bailey II. Cast: Kirk Douglas, Fredric March, Ava Gardner, Edmond O'Brien, Martin Balsam, George Macready, Whit Bissell, Hugh Marlowe, Andrew Duggan, Malcolm Atterbury, John Houseman, Colette Jackson.

1965
42 *The Train.* Jules Bricken Production (United Artists). John Frankenheimer. Franklin Coen and Frank Davis, based on *Le Front de l'Art* by Rose Valland. Cast: Paul Scofield, Jeanne Moreau, Michel Simon, Suzanne Flon, Albert Remy.
43. *The Hallelujah Trail.* Mirisch-Kappa Production (United Artists). John Sturges. John Gay, based on the novel by Bill Gulick. Cast: Lee Remick, Jim Hutton, Pamela Tiffin, Donald Pleasance, Brian Keith, Martin Landau, Dub Taylor, Whit Bissell, Val Avery. Colour.

All remaining movies are in colour

1966
44. *The Professionals.* Columbia. Richard Brooks. Richard Brooks, based on the novel by Frank O'Rourke. Cast: Lee Marvin, Robert Ryan, Claudia Cardinale, Jack Palance, Ralph Bellamy, Woody Strode.

1968

45. *The Scalphunters*. Levy-Gardner-Laven (United Artists). Sidney Pollack. William Norton. Cast: Shelley Winters, Telly Savalas, Ossie Davis, Dabney Coleman, Nick Cravat.

46. *The Swimmer*. Columbia. Frank Perry. Eleanor Perry, based on the *New Yorker* story by John Cheever. Cast: Janet Landgard, Janice Rule, Marge Champion, Cornelia Otis Skinner, Kim Hunter, Diana Muldaur, Joan Rivers, John Garfield Jnr, House Jameson, Jan Miner, Dolph Sweet, Louise Troy, Diana Van de Vlis, Rose Gregorio. Score by Marvin Hamlisch.

1969

47. *Castle Keep*. Columbia. Sidney Pollack. Daniel Taradash and David Rayfiel, based on the novel by William Eastlake. Cast: Patrick O'Neal, Jean-Pierre Aumont, Peter Falk, Scott Wilson, Tony Bill, Al Freeman Jnr, Bruce Dern, Michael Conrad.

48. *The Gypsy Moths*. MGM. John Frankenheimer. William Hanley, based on the novel by James Drought. Cast: Deborah Kerr, Gene Hackman, Scott Wilson, Sheree North, William Windom, Bonnie Bedelia.

1970

49. *Airport*. Universal. George Seaton. George Seaton, based on the novel by Arthur Hailey. Cast: Dean Martin, Jacqueline Bissett, Jean Seberg, George Kennedy, Helen Hayes, Van Heflin, Maureen Stapleton, Barry Nelson, Dana Wynter, Barbara Hale, Lloyd Nolan. Hayes won the Supporting Actress Oscar, and Stapleton was nominated for the same award. *Airport* was nominated for Best Picture.

1971

50. *Valdez is Coming.* Ira Steiner Production (United Artists). Edwin Sherin. Roland Kibbee and David Rayfiel, based on the novel by Elmore Leonard. Cast: Susan Clark, Jon Cypher, Barton Heyman, Richard Jordan, Hector Elizondo.

51. *Lawman.* Michael Winner Production (United Artists). Michael Winner. Gerald Wilson. Cast: Robert Ryan, Lee J. Cobb, Sheree North, Joseph Wiseman, Robert Duvall, Albert Salmi, J. D. Cannon, John McGiver, Richard Jordan, John Beck.

1972

52. *Ulzana's Raid.* Universal. Robert Aldrich. Alan Sharp. Cast: Bruce Davison, Jorge Lucke, Richard Jaeckel, Lloyd Bochner.

1973

53. *Scorpio.* Scimitar Films Production (United Artists). Michael Winner. David W. Rintels and Gerald Wilson, based on the story by Rintels. Cast: Alain Delon, Paul Scofield, John Colicos, Gayle Hunnicutt, J. D. Cannon.

1974

54. *Executive Action.* National General. David Miller. Dalton Trumbo, based on the story by Donald Freed. Cast: Robert Ryan, Will Geer.

55. *The Midnight Man.* Universal, 1974. Burt Lancaster and Roland Kibbee. Burt Lancaster and Roland Kibbee, based on the novel by David Anthony. Cast: Susan Clark, Cameron Mitchell, Morgan Woodward, Harris Yulin, Catherine Bach, Ed Lauter.

1975

56. *Moses, the Lawgiver*. Lew Grade, CBC and CBS-TV. Gianfranco di Bosio. Six-part, twelve-hour series for television, later condensed to a two-hour movie. Anthony Burgess *et al.* Cast: Anthony Quayle, Irene Papas, William Lancaster.

57. *Gruppo Di Famiglia in Un Interno (Conversation Piece)*. Luchino Visconti. Luchino Visconti. Cast: Silvana Magnano, Helmut Berger, Claudia Cardinale.

1976

58. *The Cassandra Crossing*. Lew Grade/Carlo Ponti – Associated General Films – International Cine Productions (Twentieth Century–Fox). George Pan Cosmatos. Tom Mankiewicz, Robert Pan and George Pan Cosmatos. Cast: Richard Harris, Ava Gardner, Sophia Loren, Martin Sheen, Ingrid Thulin, Lee Strasberg, Ann Turkel, Lionel Stander. Music by Jerry Goldsmith.

59. *Buffalo Bill and the Indians*. Robert Altman. Robert Altman and Alan Rudolph, based on the play *Indians* by Arthur Kopit. Cast: Paul Newman, Joel Grey, Geraldine Chaplin, Kevin McCarthy, Harvey Keitel, Denver Pyle, John Considine, Pat McCormick, Shelley Duvall.

60. *Victory at Entebbe*. Marvin J. Chomsky. Ernest Kinoy. Taped for television, later converted to film. Anthony Hopkins, Elizabeth Taylor, Helen Hayes, Linda Blair, Helmut Berger, Kirk Douglas, Richard Dreyfuss, Theodore Bikel, Jessica Walter, David Groh.

1977

61. *1900 (Novecento)*. Bernardo Bertolucci. Bernardo Bertolucci, Franco Arcalli and Giuseppe Bertolucci. Cast: Robert De Niro, Gerard Depardieu, Dominique Sanda, Donald Sutherland, Sterling Hayden, Alida Valli.

62. *The Island of Dr Moreau*. American International. Don Taylor. John Herman Shaner and Al Ramrus, based on the novel by H. G. Wells (Re-make). Cast: Michael York, Barbara Carrera, Nigel Davenport, Richard Baseheart, Nick Cravat.

63. *Twilight's Last Gleaming*. Lorimar. Robert Aldrich. Ronald M. Cohen and Edward Huebsch, from the novel by Walter Wager. Cast: Richard Widmark, Charles Durning, Melvyn Douglas, Paul Winfield, Burt Young, Joseph Cotten.

1978

64. *Go Tell the Spartans*. Mar Vista Productions. Ted Post. Wendell Mayes, based on the novel *Incident at Muc Wa* by Daniel Ford. Cast: Craig Wasson, Jonathan Goldsmith, Joe Unger, Dennis Howard, David Clenner, Evan King, Dolph Sweet.

1979

65. *Zulu Dawn*. A Samarkand Production. Douglas Hickox. Cy Endfield and Anthony Storey. Cast: Peter O'Toole, Simon Ward, Nigel Davenport, Michael Jayston, Peter Vaughn, James Faulkner, Christopher Cazenove, Anna Calder-Marshall, Freddie Jones, Denholm Elliott, John Mills, Bob Hoskins, Ronald Pickup. Music by Elmer Bernstein. Some dialogue was in Zulu with English subtitles.

1980

66. *Cattle Annie and Little Britches*. Lamont Johnson. Robert Ward and David Eyre. Cast: Diane Lane, Amanda Plummer, Rod Steiger, Scott Glenn, John Savage.

1981

67. *Atlantic City.* Paramount. Louis Malle. John Guare. Cast: Susan Sarandon, Kate Reid. Lancaster won his fourth New York Film Critics Best Actor Award, plus Best Actor Awards from the National Society of Film Critics, the Los Angeles Film Critics Association and the British Academy Award, and an Oscar nomination. *Atlantic City* was nominated as Best Picture, Sarandon for Best Actress, Malle for direction and Guare for best screenplay.

68. *La Pelle (The Skin).* Opera Film/Gaumont-Italia. Liliana Cavani. Robert Katz, from the novel by Curzio Malaparte. Cast: Claudia Cardinale, Marcello Mastroianni, Ken Marshall, Alexandra King.

1982

69. *Marco Polo.* NBC Television/RAI.

1983

70. *Local Hero.* (David Puttnam) Warner Brothers. Bill Forsyth. Cast: Peter Riegert, Denis Lawson, Fulton MacKay, Peter Capaldi, Christopher Rosycki, Jenny Seagrove, Jennifer Black.

71. *The Osterman Weekend.* 20th Century-Fox. Sam Peckinpah. Alan Sharp, based on the novel by Robert Ludlum. Cast: Rutger Hauer, John Hurt, Craig T. Nelson, Dennis Hopper, Chris Sarandon, Meg Foster, Helen Shaver.

Hecht-Lancaster films in which he did not appear

1. *The First Time,* Columbia, 1952; Frank Tashlin. Cast: Barbara Hale, Robert Cummings, Jeff Donnell.

2. *Marty,* United Artists, 1955; Delbert Mann. Cast: Ernest Borgnine, Betsy Blair. The film won four Oscars, including Best Picture, Best Actor for Borgnine, Best

Director for Mann and Best Screenplay for Paddy Chayefsky.

3. *The Bachelor Party*, United Artists, 1957. Delbert Mann. Cast: Don Murray, Carolyn Jones, E. G. Marshall, Jack Warden, Phillip Abbott, Nancy Marchand. Jones was nominated for the Best Supporting Actress Oscar.

4. *Take a Giant Step*, United Artists, 1959. Philip Leacock. Cast: Johnny Nash, Estelle Hemsley, Ruby Dee, Frederick O'Neal, Beah Richards.

Lancaster stage appearances

1. *Stars and Gripes* (European War Tour, 1942-45).

2. *A Sound of Hunting*, by Harry Brown, on Broadway, 1945.

3. *Knickerbocker Holiday*, Musical by Maxwell Anderson and Kurt Weill, San Francisco and Los Angeles, 1971.

4. *The Boys of Autumn*, by Bernard Sabath, San Francisco, 1981. With Kirk Douglas.

Bibliography

American Weekly, interview, 9 April 1961.

Bacon, James, *Hollywood is a Four-Letter Town*, New York, Avon, 1977.

Canby, Vincent, *The New York Times*, career analysis, 24 May 1981.

Chase, Chris, *The New York Times*, interview, 2 September 1983.

Christy, George, *Architectural Digest*, interview, October 1982.

Daniell, John, *Ava Gardner*, W. H. Allen, 1982.

Davis, Victor, *Daily Express*, interview, 31 January 1977.

Dewson, Lisa, *Photoplay Movies & Video* 'Life, Lancaster and Local Hero', April 1983.

Family Weekly, interview, 18 March 1962.

Gow, Gordon, *Hollywood in the Fifties*, New York, A. S. Barnes & Co. 1971.

Gow, Gordon, *Films and Filming*, interview, January 1973.

Graham, Sheilah, *Confessions of a Hollywood Columnist*. New York, William Morrow and Co., 1969.

Hall, William, *Evening News*, interview, 13 February 1968.

Hall, William, and Crawley, Tony, *Game*, interview, February 1975.

Hill, James, *Rita Hayworth: A Memoir*, New York, Simon and Schuster, 1983.

Hinxman, Margaret, *Daily Mail*, interview, 16 May 1982.

Hunter, Allan, and Astaire, Mark, *Local Hero: The Making of the Film*, Edinburgh, Polygon Books, 1983.

Huston, John, *An Open Book*, London, Macmillan Publishers Ltd, 1981.

Kearns, Michael, *Drama-Logue*, interview, 2-8 April 1981.

Lancaster, Burt, *Films and Filming*, 'Hollywood Drove Me to a Double Life', January 1962.

Lancaster, Burt, *Films Illustrated*, extracts from National Film Theatre panel appearance, September 1973.

Lochte, Dick, *Los Angeles Free Press*, interview, 8 December 1972.

Mann, Roderick, *Sunday Express*, interview, 2 July 1972.

Martin, Pete, *Saturday Evening Post*, interview, 24 June 1961.

Martin, Pete, *Saturday Evening Post*, 'Hollywood Hard Guy', September 1948.

Ottaway, Robert, *TV Times*, interview, 15 March 1973.

Pickard, Roy, *The Oscar Movies From A-Z*, Hamlyn, 1978.

Pratley, Gerald, *The Cinema of John Frankenheimer*,Tantivy Press, 1969.

Reed, Rex, *Travolta to Keaton*, New York,

Schuster, Mel, *Films in Review*, August-September 1969.

Speed, F. Maurice, ed., *Film Review 1978-79*, W. H. Allen 1978.

Stirling, Monica, *A Screen of Time: A Study of Luchino Visconti*, Harcourt Brace, Jovanovich, 1979.

Thomas, Tony, *Burt Lancaster*, New York, Pyramid, 1975.

Vermilye, Jerry, *Burt Lancaster*, New York, Falcon/Crescent, 1971.

Wallis, Hal, *Starmaker*, New York.

Weis, Elisabeth, ed, National Society of Film Critics, *The Movie Star*, New York, Viking/Penguin, 1981.

Winters, Shelley, *Shelley, Also Known as Shirley*, Granada, 1981.

Zec, Donald, *Story of Lee Marvin*, New English Library, 1979.

Index